GERMAN SKILLS FOR YOU

Jennifer Deitz

Hutchinson

London   Melbourne   Auckland   Johannesburg

Hutchinson Education

An imprint of Century Hutchinson Ltd
62–65 Chandos Place, London WC2N 4NW

Century Hutchinson Australia (Pty) Ltd
PO Box 496, 16–22 Church Street, Hawthorn, Melbourne,
Victoria 3122, Australia

Century Hutchinson New Zealand Ltd
PO Box 40-086, Glenfield, Auckland 10, New Zealand

Century Hutchinson South Africa (Pty) Ltd
PO Box 337, Bergvlei, 2012 South Africa

First published in 1988

© Jennifer Deitz, 1988

Set in Photina

by H Charlesworth & Co Ltd, Huddersfield

Printed and bound in Great Britain

British Library Cataloguing in Publication Data

Deitz, Jennifer
   German skills for you.
   1. German language — For schools
   I. Title
   438

ISBN 0-09-172925-4

Acknowledgements

The author would like to thank the following people for their help and support during the writing of this book: David Deitz, Ilka Neugebauer, staff and pupils of the Realschule Meinerzhagen, Ina Peters and Nan Fraser.

   Photographs are by permission of: David Deitz, Lesley Collier and Jennifer Deitz. Artwork by Martina Selway.

Contents

Introduction iv
Do's and Don'ts v
Topic 1: People 1
Topic 2: House and Home 11
Topic 3: School 20
Topic 4: Holidays and Travel 29
Topic 5: Travel and Transport 46
Topic 6: Free Time and Entertainment 62
Topic 7: Shopping, Food and Drink 74
Topic 8: Around the Town 96
Topic 9: At your Service 110

Introduction

German Skills for You is a book of practice material for students working towards the GCSE examination, which is based entirely on authentic materials and realistic situations. The book is divided into nine topics which cover most of the structures and vocabulary specified by the various examining groups. Each topic is divided into the four skills — reading, listening, speaking and writing — using wherever possible interesting material from authentic sources. The skills are indicated by the following symbols, which appear on the first activity in each skill section:

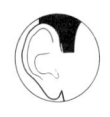

Reading   Listening   Speaking   Writing

The items in each section are ranged progressively from basic to higher. All the listening comprehension exercises have been recorded on an accompanying cassette and a complete teacher's tapescript is included in a separate booklet. *German Skills for You* can be used with any existing course book and the individual exercises may be exploited in a variety of different ways other than those suggested by the author.

About the author

Jennifer Deitz is an experienced French and German teacher, who is now Head of Modern Languages at Howden Clough High School in Batley, West Yorkshire.

Do's and Don'ts

Reading comprehension

DO — read through the whole item at least twice before attempting the question.
— read the question carefully and decide exactly what information you are looking for. Take note of the number of details the question requires and look at the mark scheme, if there is one, to see how many marks the question is worth.
— remember that there may be clues in the questions themselves and the order in which they are asked.
— look carefully at the words themselves. You may recognize a part of the word, which could set you on the correct thinking process.

DON'T — worry if you don't understand every single word of the German, some of it will probably not be required to answer the question anyway.
— leave a blank if you can help it — make a logical guess. No answer means **no** chance of any marks.

Listening comprehension

DO — read the instructions for the test carefully and note how many times you can expect to hear the information.
— read the questions carefully and bear in mind what you have to listen for when the recording is played.
— remember to give all the details necessary — the mark scheme should indicate the number of marks available for a particular question.
— make intelligent guesses if you are not sure of an answer.
— learn everyday information such as times and dates — many questions are based on information of this kind.

DON'T — panic if you do not understand some of the longer items first time around. You will probably get a second hearing of such items.
— try to write when you ought to be listening — you will miss vital pieces of information if you do.

Speaking

DO — be sure you know what kind of tasks you will have to cope with.
— take advantage of any preparation time to actually prepare what you are going to say.
— speak clearly and loud enough for your voice to record.
— say something, even if you're not too sure whether it's right or wrong.

DON'T — try to translate literally in role-play situations. Try to put yourself in the situation and think what the German person might say.
— be content to answer questions with just a "Ja" or a "Nein". The more you try to say, the better chance you will give the examiner of assessing your spoken German.

— worry about being nervous. Most people are when they have to speak in front of someone else. The person conducting the test is there to bring out the best in you, not trip you up!

Writing

DO
— make sure you know what kind of tasks you will be required to tackle in the examination room.
— read any written German through very carefully before starting to write.
— make sure you answer all questions put to you in the stimulus material.
— include all the information required of you in the question.
— try to write legibly and neatly. This will help you when you read your answer through again, and will make the examiner's task a little easier.
— share the time available equally between the tasks — if you spend too long on the first question you will end up rushing the others.

DON'T — waste time writing English words and phrases in your answer. If you can't say what you want to say in German, then don't say it at all. Write only the German you know.
— go over the number of words you have been asked to write by more than a few — otherwise you will use up too much time.

TOPIC 1: *People*

1 Happy birthday!

Here are some birthday greetings taken from a newspaper.

Herzlichen Dank

sage ich allen, die mir zu meinem

80. GEBURTSTAG

mit Glückwünschen, Blumen und Geschenken Freude bereiteten.

Anna Zaborowski

Alflen, im Mai 1986

Hurra, hurra
Petra

wird heut' 25 Jahr'.

Es gratulieren und wünschen alles Gute und Gesundheit

Dein Mann Horst
und Stefanie

Die fröhliche Guten-Tag-Anzeige

Liebe Ulli!

Jemand zu vergessen, den man mag, ist schwer,
jemand zu vergessen, den man lieb hat, ist schwerer,
jemanden zu vergessen, den man liebt,
ist am schwersten.
Doch Dich zu vergessen, ist unmöglich!

Zu Deinem 21. Geburtstag alles Liebe und Gute

Dein Schatz Heinr. . . .

Bianca
zum 18. Geburtstag

Nie verlerne so zu lachen
wie Du jetzt lachst, froh und frei,
denn ein Leben ohne Lachen
ist ein Frühling ohne Mai.

Deine Oma

---

1 Who is wishing Petra a happy birthday?
2 What else do they wish for her?
3 How old is Ulli today?
4 Who is wishing Bianca a happy birthday?
5 For what three things is Anna saying thank you?

2 Exchange partners

Here are some extracts from letters to an English school which is about to set up an exchange with a German school.

Read each extract carefully, then fill in the table for each person.

A Name: **Cordula Zahlten**
Geburtsdatum: 6. 10. 75
Ich bin 1.70 m groß, habe braune Haare und braune Augen.
Ich habe noch einen vier Jahre älteren Bruder.
Meine Hobbys sind: Ski-fahren, Fußball spielen und sonstige Sportarten.

B Ich heiße **Stefan** und bin am 31.5. in Gummersbach geboren.
Ich bin 1.65 m groß, habe hellblonde Haare und grüne Augen.
Meine Hobbys sind Computer, Musik hören, Fußball und andere Sportarten. Fußball spiele ich in einem Verein. Wir sind eine sportliche Familie — mein Vater spielt Tennis, meine Mutter schwimmt gern, und mein Bruder fährt gern Ski.

C Mein Name ist **Sven**. Ich bin 14 Jahre alt und besuche die neunte Klasse der Realschule. Ich bin ziemlich groß, habe braune Haare und blaue Augen und trage eine Brille. Ich bin sehr freundlich. Meine Hobbys sind Schießen und Musik hören, Computer und Radfahren. Meine Mutter ist im Moment arbeitslos. Mein Vater ist Fabrikarbeiter. Ich habe zwei Brüder — sie sind jünger als ich.

Name	Age or birthday	Brothers and sisters	Physical description	Hobbies
CORDULA				
STEFAN				
SVEN				

3 Wanted!

These details have been taken from police posters.

A

> Das Bundeskriminalamt bittet um Mithilfe.
>
> **BKA**
>
> **20,000 DM BELOHNUNG**
>
> Mit Haftbefehl gesucht wird
> UDO ALBRECHT
>
> 46 Jahre alt
> etwa 178 cm groß
> braune Augen
> trägt zeitweise eine Perücke.
>
> Udo Albrecht wird wegen der Begehung eines Bankraubs mit Haftbefehl gesucht.
>
> Hinweise an das Bundeskriminalamt Meckenheim. Tel. 0 22 25/90-0

1. Describe the man the police are looking for.
2. Why are they looking for him?

B

> Das Bundeskriminalamt bittet um Mithilfe.
>
> **BKA**
>
> Gesucht wird
> **INGE SCHMID**
>
> 33 Jahre alt
> 165 cm groß
> grüne Augen
> lockige braune Haare
> trägt zeitweise eine Brille
>
> Ingemar Schmid wird wegen Autodiebstahls gesucht.
> Hinweise an das Bundeskriminalamt Meckenheim. Tel. 0 22 25/90-0

1. Describe Inge Schmid's hair.
2. What colour are her eyes?
3. Why do the police want to question her?

4 Where are they now?

Here are three items from a German magazine from people who wish to get in touch with someone they have recently seen or met, but do not have an address for.

> Wir suchen die **Jungs**, die am **15. Dezember '86** in **Frankfurt-Stadtmitte** bei **McDonald's** standen. Ihr wart alle zwischen 15 und 17 und hattet **ausgeflippte** Sachen an. Wir sind die zwei Mädchen, die Ihr so angeglotzt habt. Meldet Euch bitte beim Treffpunkt, dort bekommt Ihr unsere Adresse

A 1 Who is looking for whom?
    2 When and where did they see each other?

> Wir suchen die Jungs, die am **25. November '86** in **Rendsburg** waren. Ihr hattet **Jeans** und **graue Daunenjacken** an und habt **blonde Haare**. Einer von Euch hat bei Karstadt **Turnschuhe** anprobiert. Wir sind die **Mädchen** mit den **blauen Daunenjacken**. Meldet Euch bei Beate Rathje.

B 1 How does Beate describe the boys she is looking for?
    2 What colour were the quilted jackets the boys were wearing?
    3 How will the boys know which girls are looking for them?

> Ich suche den **Jungen**, der am 15. November '86 beim **Sportlerball** (Disco) in **Geradstetten** mit mir getanzt hat. Leider mußte ich mit meinen Freundinnen nach Hause fahren und konnte Dich nicht nach Deinem Namen fragen. Du hast **blonde, kurze Haare** und bist **schlank**. Wenn Du Dich an mich erinnerst, schreib an: Melanie Brändle, Olgastraße 30,

C 1 Where had Melanie met the boy she is looking for?
    2 Why was she unable to get his name and address earlier?
    3 Describe the boy.
    4 What does she ask the boy to do?

5 Tennis idol Steffi Graf

Steffi Graf wurde 1969 geboren. Sie ist 1.73 m groß und wiegt 56 Kilo. Sie hat ziemlich lange blonde Haare und ist ein freundliches und ruhiges Mädchen. Peter Graf ist ihr Vater, Trainer und Manager, und er ist sehr stolz auf seine Tochter. Als Steffi 4 Jahre alt war, spielte er mit ihr Tennis im Keller und im Wohnzimmer.

Steffi wohnt mit ihrer Mutter und ihrem Vater in Bühl bei Heidelberg. Sie hat zwei Hunde — einen Boxerhund, Ben, und einen Schäferhund, Max. Sie spielt gern mit den Hunden und liest gern.

1 How old is Steffi?
2 What is her hair like?
3 How old was she when she first began to play tennis?
4 Where does she live?
5 What does she like doing?

1 German people talk about themselves

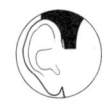

A Listen to the recording, then fill in this table about Barbara.

Birthdate	
Hometown	
Occupation	
Hair colour	
Eye colour	
Height	
Weight	
Favourite clothes	

B Answer these questions about Kurt.
1 How old is Kurt?
2 What colour are his eyes?
3 How long has he been living in England?
4 In addition to listening to music, what else does he like doing?
5 How often does he go jogging?

C Listen to the recording, then write down as many things as you can about Susanne.

D Answer these questions about Ingo.
1 How old is he?
2 Who else lives in the flat with him?
3 What does he often have to do in the afternoon?
4 What sport does he like to play?

E After listening to the recording, decide which of these statements are true.
1 Emine lives in Turkey.
2 There are five more children in the family besides Emine.
3 She is tall and slim.
4 She has long brown hair.

2 Attack in Frankfurt

Listen to this recording of a news item about two men wanted for questioning by the police in connection with a serious attack.

1. When did the attack take place?
2. Who was attacked?

Look carefully at these descriptions of the two men, listen to the tape again, and tick the statements which you think are correct.

First man	✓?
height about 170 cm	
aged 30-ish	
round face	
light blond hair	
had beard	

Second man	✓?
older than 1st man	
short black hair	
glasses	
wore blue anorak and jeans	
had beard and moustache	

3 A Turkish boy talks about himself

Part 1

Answer these questions in English about Remzi.

1. How old is Remzi?
2. Where does he live now?
3. How old was Remzi when his father left Turkey?
4. How long has Remzi actually lived in Germany?
5. Why did he find schoolwork difficult at first?
6. What is his favourite subject?
7. What would he like to do when he leaves school?

Part 2

Listen to the rest of what Remzi has to say, then decide which of the following statements are true.

1. The Religious Festival of Kurban lasts for four days.
2. The family goes to the Mosque to sing.
3. The children get new clothes from their parents.
4. Ramadan lasts about a month.
5. Remzi finds fasting very easy.
6. The children receive toys from their relatives at the end of Ramadan.

1 Names and addresses

On a visit to your penfriend in Germany, one of his/her friends asks if he/she can have your full name and address so that he/she can write to you. Imagine this conversation with a partner.

Person A (German)	*Person B (Visitor)*
1 Wie ist dein Name?	1 Tell him/her your name.
2 Wie buchstabiert man das?	2 Tell him/her how you spell it.
3 Wie ist deine Adresse?	3 Tell him/her your address.

Now you play the part of Person A and find out his/her details.

2 Talking to grandmother

You are introduced to your penfriend's grandmother. The following conversation takes place. Take it in turns with a partner to play the part of the Grandma.

Grandma: Asks how old you are.
You: Say your age.
Grandma: Asks if you have brothers and sisters.
You: Tell her.
Grandma: Asks where you live.
You: Tell her.

3 My family

You have been showing some snapshots of your family to your penfriend's mum. She asks you some questions about your family.

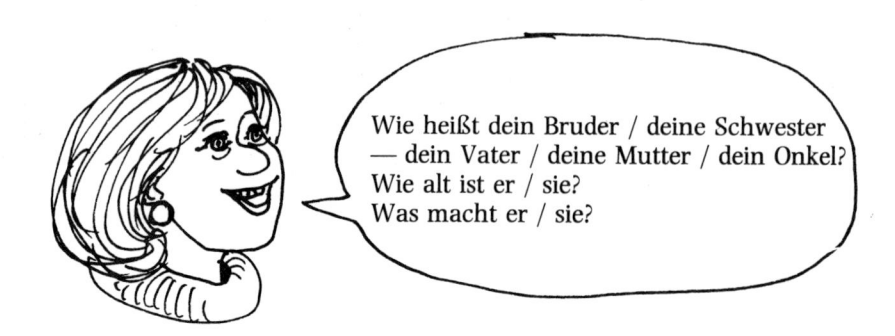

> Wie heißt dein Bruder / deine Schwester
> — dein Vater / deine Mutter / dein Onkel?
> Wie alt ist er / sie?
> Was macht er / sie?

With a partner take it in turn to ask the questions and give the answers. Write down any more questions you could ask.

4 Penfriends

Your teacher is sending a tape recording to a German school for you and some of your friends who want to make contact with German teenagers. You do the recording in German and your teacher asks you to talk for a minute or so about yourself and your family. Try to give as much information as possible in this time.

5 Description 1

You have spent the day in school with your penfriend and have met lots of his/her friends. Unfortunately you cannot remember all their names. One boy/girl was particularly nice to you and you would like to meet him/her again — but what was he/she called? In desperation you describe him/her to your penfriend.

Tell your penfriend what the boy/girl looked like and what he/she was wearing that day.

6 Description 2

You have been cycling in the German town where you are staying. You decide to have a look inside the church and leave your bike propped up outside. When you come out you are just in time to see your bike being ridden off by a youth aged about 16, with black hair and wearing a blue shirt and jeans. You rush to the police station to report the loss and to give a description of the youth.

1 Filling in a form

Your German friend is a keen swimmer and takes you along to the local swimming club. The leader is pleased to see you and asks you to fill in this form for club records. Please don't write in this book!

```
           GELSENHEIMER SCHWIMMVEREIN

   Name:            ............................
   Vorname:         ............................
   Wohnort:         ............................
   Straße:          ............................
   Hausnummer:      ............................
   Telefonnummer:   ............................
   Geburtsdatum:    ............................
   Geschwister:     ............................
   Elternname:      ............................
```

2 First letter to a penfriend

These requests for penfriends were taken from a German teenage magazine. Choose one and write a reply, explaining where you live, what you look like and stating one activity you like doing.

Ich bin 15 und suche Briefkontakt mit Jungen und Mädchen zwischen 13 und 16. Hobbys: Fußball, Tennis, Kino und Musik. Briefe mit Foto werden garantiert beantwortet. Michael Dietrich, Am Hüttberg 6,

Welcher Junge hat Lust, einem 14jährigen Mädchen zu schreiben? Hobbys: Reiten, Schwimmen, Tanzen... Schreibt bitte mit Foto an: Anja Winter, Töpferstraße 8,

Ich bin 16 und suche Brieffreundinnen zwischen 14 und 18. Hobbys: Tennis, Kino und Musik. Späteres Kennenlernen nicht ausgeschlossen. Schreibt bitte mit Foto an: Thomas Apitzsch, Buddestraße 36.

3 My family and where I live

Your penfriend asks you to write a piece in German for the school magazine about yourself and your family. In 100 words give some information about your parents, your brothers and sisters and where you live.

TOPIC 2: House and Home

1 My house

In this extract from a letter, Grete, a German girl, describes her house.

> ... Jetzt beschreibe ich Dir unser Haus. Meine Eltern haben es vor zehn Jahren gekauft, als es ganz neu war. Es ist ein Zweifamilienhaus und befindet sich am Rande des Dorfes, wo es sehr ruhig ist.
> Im Keller sind die Zentralheizung für das ganze Haus, ein Abstellraum, ein Waschraum und eine Dusche.
> Im Erdgeschoß wohnen unsere Mieter, Herr und Frau Koch. Unsere Wohnung ist im ersten Stock. Dort sind ein Wohnzimmer, ein Eßzimmer, eine Küche, das Schlafzimmer meiner Eltern und ein Badezimmer mit Toilette.
> Mein Zimmer und das meiner Schwester sind im zweiten Stock. Dort ist auch ein kleiner Hobbyraum, wo meine Mutter ihre Nähmaschine hat. Hier ist ein Foto meines Hauses ...

1. How old is the house?
2. How many families live there?
3. On which floor do Herr and Frau Koch live?
4. What is in the cellar?
5. What is on the first floor?
6. Where is Grete's bedroom?
7. In addition to the bedroom, what else is on the second floor?

2 Moving house?

Your penfriend's family is thinking about moving house. All of you consult the small advertisements in the newspaper, but no one can agree!

a   Frau Glotzbach would like to move to a large farmhouse with plenty of land, where she can grow all her own vegetables.
b   Herr Glotzbach thinks that would be far too expensive and would settle for something old with a garage for his new car.
c   Your penfriend's elder brother is hoping to go to university soon and would like to rent a room in the town centre.
d   Your penfriend will move anywhere — provided there is no garden, because he/she hates digging.

Here is a selection of the advertisements they looked at. Match up each advertisement with each member of the family.

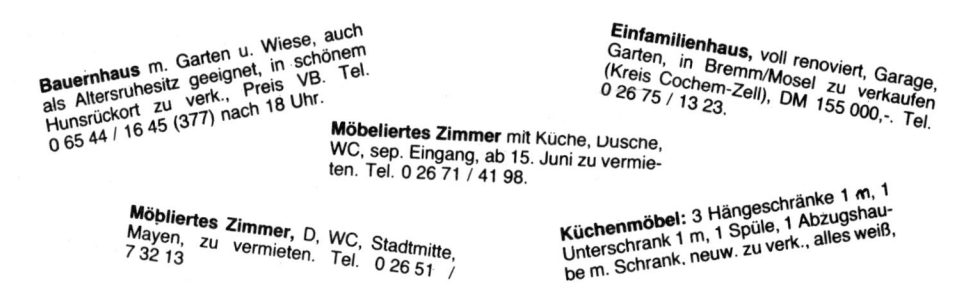

Bauernhaus m. Garten u. Wiese, auch als Altersruhesitz geeignet, in schönem Hunsrückort zu verk., Preis VB. Tel. 0 65 44 / 16 45 (377) nach 18 Uhr.

Einfamilienhaus, voll renoviert, Garage, Garten, in Bremm/Mosel zu verkaufen (Kreis Cochem-Zell), DM 155 000,-. Tel. 0 26 75 / 13 23.

Möbeliertes Zimmer mit Küche, Dusche, WC, sep. Eingang, ab 15. Juni zu vermieten. Tel. 0 26 71 / 41 98.

Möbliertes Zimmer, D, WC, Stadtmitte, Mayen, zu vermieten. Tel. 0 26 51 / 7 32 13

Küchenmöbel: 3 Hängeschränke 1 m, 1 Unterschrank 1 m, 1 Spüle, 1 Abzugshaube m. Schrank. neuw. zu verk., alles weiß,

3 Alterations

The Glotzbachs think they might do better to stay where they are after all and decide to make some alterations to their present house. You make a list of some of the things that need doing and you look for firms advertising such services in the paper. Which firm will do which job?

1   New doors and windows.
2   A new heating system.
3   New furniture.
4   New carpets.
5   New fitted cupboards.

baumit-REGALE Einbau-, Schrank- und Bücherwände vielseitig, formschön, preiswert für jeden Raum. Prospekte sendet: **baumit** 2807 Achim 10 Postf.124

TEPPICHHAUS Farben Müller COCHEM Nur Endertstr. 80 - An der Sesselbahn

BRETZ Fachbetrieb für Metallbau Heizung · Sanitär Fenster und Türen 0 26 53 **60 11** KUNDENDIENST für Heizung- & Sanitäranlagen

Willkommen zum Bauherren-Treff. Fenster und Haustüren *live* Besuchen Sie unsere ständige Musterausstellung **bretz** Kaisersesch, Am Bahnhof, Tel. 02653/205

Einrichtungshaus Reuter Kaisersesch, Bahnhstr. 41-45, Tel. 0 26 53 60 88   Möbel — Dekorationen — Bodenbeläge Bahnhofstraße 41 - 45   0 26 53 **60 88**

4 My bedroom

Konrad describes in his letter his newly-decorated bedroom.

  ... *Mein Schlafzimmer sieht jetzt ganz toll aus. Ich habe es fast selbst gemacht — Vati hat nur die Tür und das Fenster gestrichen. Sie sind weiß; Mutti sagt, weiß sehe immer so sauber aus. Die Wände haben wir blau gestrichen. Die Vorhänge und der Teppich sind dunkelblau.*

  Vor dem Fenster ist der Schreibtisch, wo ich jetzt diesen Brief schreibe. Neben der Tür ist das Bücherregal, das ich selbst gemacht habe und der neue Schrank, den wir letzten Freitag gekauft haben. Neben dem Bett auf einem kleinen Tisch ist meine Stereoanlage ...

1 Who has decorated Konrad's bedroom?
2 What colour are the door and window?
3 What items in the room are dark blue?
4 What does Konrad say about the bookcase?
5 Where exactly is his stereo unit?

5 My home in Germany

A German teacher spending some time in England describes her German home for her English pupils.

  "*Mein Mann und ich wohnen in einem großen Haus, einem Bungalow, der mitten in einem hübschen Garten und alten Bäumen liegt, weitab von der Straße. Wir müssen einen langen schmalen Privatweg entlangfahren, um in die Doppelgarage zu gelangen.*

  Der Eingang zum Haus ist überdacht. Von der Eingangshalle gehen die Garderobe mit Gästetoilette, die Küche und die Tür zur Kellertreppe ab. Von dort betritt man auch den großen Wohnraum. Vor dem Kamin steht eine Sitzgruppe mit drei niedrigen Couchtischen für 8 bis 10 Personen. Eine kleinere Sitzgruppe befindet sich vor der Terrassentür. Alle Wohnzimmerfenster haben eine Markise, die gleichzeitig unsere Terrasse im Sommer überdacht, wo wir mit ca.8 Personen sitzen oder uns sonnen können.

  An das Wohnzimmer schließt sich ein Eßzimmer an. Außerdem gelangt man vom Wohnzimmer aus in den Schlaftrakt mit 2 Schlafzimmern, einem Arbeitszimmer, einem Badezimmer und Toilette, Dusche, Badewanne und einem Doppelwaschbecken.

Unser Haus ist völlig unterkellert. Im Keller liegen die Waschküche, der Heizungskeller, der Vorratskeller, der Tischtennis— oder Hobbyraum und der Weinkeller.

Übrigens kann man vom Keller aus in einen Teil des Gartens gelangen, wo ein runder Sandkasten ist und das Hundehaus steht, in dem unser Bernhardiner wohnt.

Da das Haus kein Flachdach sondern ein Walmdach besitzt, kann man auf dem Boden überall stehen oder große Schränke aufstellen.

Der Bungalow hat eine Gesamtwohnfläche von 140 m^2."

1 Where is this house situated?
2 What rooms open off the hallway?
3 Where are the settees in the living room?
4 How many bedrooms are there?
5 What else is there in this part of the house besides the bedrooms?
6 What can be found in the large cellar area?
7 In which part of the garden is the dog kennel?
8 What does the house owner think the advantages are of having a high roof to the bungalow, rather than a flat one?

1 Uwe describes his home

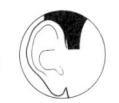

1. What kind of house does Uwe live in?
2. What is on the ground floor?
3. How many rooms are there on the first floor?
4. What does he say about the outside of the house?
5. Where is the house situated?

2 Barbara describes her student accommodation

Answer true or false to the following statements.

1. Barbara has a room in the cellar of a bungalow.
2. She rents the room.
3. She has her own bath and toilet.
4. The bungalow is right in the centre of Heidelberg.
5. She walks to the university.

3 Susanne's room

Fill in this table about where Susanne lives.

Number of people in house	
Number of bathrooms	
Cost of Susanne's room	
Distance from her office	

4 The Neugebauer family introduce themselves

Part 1

Listen to the recordings of Herr and Frau Neugebauer, then fill in this table.

Name	Age	Job	Transport to work
Frau Neugebauer			
Herr Neugebauer			

Part 2

Now listen to the recordings made by Katja and Ilka and complete this table.

Name	Age	University	Subjects	Hobbies
Katja				
Ilka				

Part 3

Listen to what Frau Klara Neugebauer has to say, then answer these questions.

1 How old is she?
2 What does she describe herself as?
3 What does she say about her family?
4 How many grandchildren does she have?
5 What happens on special holidays?
6 What does Frau Neugebauer do on such occasions?

16

1 Where I live

You are talking to your penfriend about your home.
   With a partner act out the following situation — take it in turns to be the penfriend.

Penfriend	You
Wohnst du in einem Haus oder in einer Wohnung?	Tell him/her where you live.
Ist dein Haus/deine Wohnung klein oder groß?	Tell him/her how big your house/flat is.
Gibt es einen Garten?	Tell him/her whether or not you have a garden.

2 My bedroom

Your penfriend wants to know about your bedroom. He/she asks you these questions — how would you answer?

1 Wie groß ist dein Schlafzimmer?
2 Hast du dein eigenes Zimmer?
3 Welche Farbe ist die Tür?
4 Wieviele Poster hast du?
5 Wer hat dein Schlafzimmer gestrichen?
6 Gefällt dir dein Schlafzimmer? Warum oder warum nicht?

3 A typical house

Whilst you are in school with your German penfriend, the teacher asks you to describe, in German, a typical home in Britain. You decide to describe your own. What would you say?

4 An interview

What questions would you ask a non-English speaking German to find out where he/she lives and what his/her house looks like? Use any of the questions you have come across in this topic to help you.

1 All about my home

Look at the extract of the letter, on page 11, from the German girl, in the reading section of this unit. Write back to her telling her all about your home — where it is, how many rooms it has, etc.

2 My bedroom

Write back to Konrad (from My bedroom, on page 13) describing your bedroom. Say what's in it, what colour it is, the colour of the door, window, carpet, curtains, etc.

3 Our new house

Imagine you are one of the people moving house in the story suggested by the series of pictures shown here.

4 Buying a new house

Imagine that you and your family are shortly to move house. Here are details of the new house your family has bought. Write a letter in German to your penfriend telling him/her all about it.

DESCRIPTION: AN ATTRACTIVE BRICK BUILT SEMI DETACHED HOUSE situated in this extremely popular location, in a much sought after residential area. This property would suit both the couple or young family and benefits from having a GAS FIRED CENTRAL HEATING SYSTEM.

The accommodation briefly comprises: entrance hall, downstairs cloaks/w.c., spacious through lounge, with dining area, kitchen, 3 bedrooms, bathroom/w.c. with a fitted shower unit. Outside the house are average sized gardens to the front and rear and a brick built garage with an up and over door.

DIRECTIONS: From Leeds City Centre travelling out onto Harrogate Road at the roundabout and junction with the Leeds Ring Road carry straight on to the dual carriageway. Take the approx. 5th turning on the left hand side into Primley Park View, carry on and turn 3rd left into Primley Park Drive.

TOPIC 3: *School*

1 My school

"Ich besuche eine Gesamtschule. Die Schule befindet sich in einem kleinen Dorf in der Nähe von Fulda und liegt am Rande des Dorfes auf einem Hügel.

Die Schule sieht ganz modern aus und ist ziemlich groß. Die Klassenzimmer sind groß und hell. Ich finde das Gebäude ganz schön."

1 What kind of school does this person go to?
2 Where exactly is the school?
3 What does the school look like?
4 What does he say about the classrooms and the school in general?

2 Timetable for Class 9d

Look at the timetable at the top of the next page and answer these questions.

1 How long does each lesson last in this school?
2 How many lessons are there each weekday?
3 How many times a week does this class have geography?
4 What two afternoon lessons are there?
5 What is the third lesson on Wednesday?
6 How many sciences are studied?
7 How many foreign languages does this class learn?

Zeit	Montag	Dienstag	Mittwoch	Donnerstag	Freitag	Samstag
7:40 - 8:25	Geschichte	Mathematik	Englisch	AG: ↓	Physik	Englisch
8:30 - 9:15	Deutsch	Religion	Politik	Informatik	Biologie	"
9:35 - 10:20	Physik	Deutsch	Deutsch	Physik	Deutsch	Mathem.-
10:25 - 11:10	Biologie	Erdkunde	Geschichte	Biologie	Erdkunde	"
11:25 - 12:10	Musik	Chemie	Religion	Mathematik	Sport	
12:15 - 13:00	Kunst	Englisch	Chemie	Geschichte	"	
		Hauswirt-schaft				
				Volleyball		

3 School report for Thomas Johann

1. How many subjects does Thomas study?
2. In most of his subjects Thomas's work is satisfactory, but at which two does he need to work harder?
3. Thomas's mum signed the report before it was returned to school, but who else (positions, not names) signed it before he got it?
4. There is a date on the report 30.1.88 — to what does it refer?

4 School report for Karin Lock

This report came from a school in Cologne.
Answer true or false to these statements about Karin's report.

1. She studies 15 subjects.
2. She needs to work harder at music.
3. Her best subjects are religion, history and French.
4. The report was issued on 12 November 1987.
5. School starts again on 8 November 1987.
6. Karin studies three foreign languages.

5 Extra help: 1

Your penfriend has not had very good marks recently for tests in some of his/her subjects. His/her parents have discussed the idea of him/her having extra lessons (Nachhilfeunterricht) in some subjects. You look in the local newspaper to see what's on offer.

1 Which advertisement offers extra help in English and German?
2 Which number would you telephone if you wanted to learn to play the guitar?
3 Your penfriend is in the 10th class at school — why would there be no point in contacting the person in advertisement **a**?
4 Which advertisement has been placed by someone looking for extra help in maths and English?

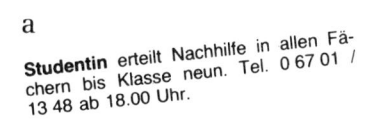

a
Studentin erteilt Nachhilfe in allen Fächern bis Klasse neun. Tel. 0 67 01 / 13 48 ab 18.00 Uhr.

c **Suche Nachhilfeunterricht** in Englisch + Mathematik, 6. Schuljahr, Gymn., Tel. 0 26 51 / 28 60

b **Unterricht**
Musikunterricht i. Gitarre, Klarinette, Sysophon. Komme ev. zu Ihnen. Tel. 0 67 43 / 68 51

d **Suche für Mathe Nachhilfe,** Grundschule. Zuschriften unter Chiffre-Nr. S-357572 an den Verlag.

e **Intensivnachhilfe**
Engl./Deutsch, alle Schularten, bis zum Abitur erteilt Sprachl. m. langj. Unterrichtserf. (in Mayen)
Tel. 0 26 51 / 64 42

6 Extra help: 2

Whilst looking through the newspaper, you see a large section of advertising devoted to the learning of foreign languages.

1 How many hours of tuition would you get if you went to learn Italian in Italy?
2 What kind of accommodation is available to people who want to come to England to learn English?
3 How long does the 'English in the Sun' course last?
4 What kind of accommodation is offered in Spain?
5 List the other foreign languages on offer in addition to the ones already mentioned.

Intensiv-Sprachkurse im Ausland

Englisch/Amerikanisch-Französisch-Spanisch
Italienisch-Niederländisch
Portugiesisch/Brasilianisch

Unterrichtstermine das ganze Jahr hindurch, anerkennungsfähig für Bildungsurlaub.

- für Erwachsene aller Berufs- und Altersgruppen
- für lernwillige Oberstufenschüler (kein Schüler-Ferien-Tourismus)
- Kleingruppen-Unterricht, zwei bis acht Wochen
- Einzel-Unterricht, eins bis vier Wochen
- Feriensprachkurse „English in the Sun", zwei bis vier Wochen

Prospekt und individuelle Beratung kostenlos durch

AUSLAND SPRACHENDIENST GMBH
Hegelstraße 52 B, 6072 Dreieich bei Frankfurt/M.
Telefon (0 61 03) 3 41 13, Telex 417 960 as d
Fachorganisation für qualifizierte Sprachschulung im Ausland

Englisch in England

Intensiv- und Spracherholungskurse durch englische Lehrerin mit langjähriger Erfahrung an deutschen Schulen. Kleiner Kreis, persönliche Atmosphäre. Unterbringung im eigenen Haus am Meer oder bei Gastfamilien, Schülerferienkurse, Abiturvorbereitung, Cambridge Certificate, Anfänger und Fortgeschrittene, Wirtschaftsführungskräfte.
Janet Muth-Dunford, Am Mühlenberg 38, 4800 Bielefeld 1, ☎ (05 21) 10 12 53

ITALIENISCH IN ITALIEN

Intensivkurs Italienisch- alle Schwierigkeitsgrade- in Padua.
Ein Monat: Unterricht (80 Stunden) und Unterkunft: DM 930.

ISTITUTO CULTURALE
BERTRAND RUSSELL
Via Cavour 1 - 35100 PADOVA
ITALIEN - Tel. (49) 654051

ANDALUSIEN

Ferienkurs für spanische Sprache und andalusische Kultur GRANADA 10.-28. 9. 84 Intensivkurs, kleine Gruppen, einzigart. Informationsprogramm, Exkursionen, Unterkunft in Familie od. Hotel, ab DM 490,–
INFORMATION: AFIB – Arbeitsgemeinschaft für interkulturelle Begegnung e. V., Melbweg 36a, 5300 Bonn 1, Tel. (02 28) 46 49 21

1 Complete the timetable

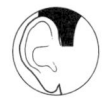

Here is Josef's school timetable, but only partly filled in. Listen carefully to the tape and fill in the gaps.

Give the English names of the missing subjects 1–9. What does Josef say about Saturdays?

Zeit	Montag	Dienstag	Mittwoch	Donnerstag	Freitag	Samstag
8:10 – 8:55	Geschichte	(2)	(5)	Wirtschaft	Latein	
8:55 – 9:40	Biologie	Biologie	Latein	Deutsch	Geometrie	
9:45 – 10:30	Englisch	Algebra	Geometrie	Englisch	Erdkunde	
10:55 – 11:40	Deutsch	(3)	(6)	Algebra	(8)	
11:45 – 12:30	Kunst	(4)	Religion	Latein	(9)	
12:30 – 13:15	(1)	Physik	(7)	Sport	Englisch	

2 Favourite subjects: 1

Several pupils were asked about their favourite school subjects. Listen carefully to their replies.

For each person, write down in English the school subject(s) mentioned.

1 Bernd
2 Birgit
3 Kurt
4 Heike
5 Martina

3 Favourite subjects: 2

Christoph, Helene and Richard talk about school subjects.

1 Which subjects does Christoph like?
2 What does he like doing in his spare time?
3 What job would he like to do and why?

1 What is Helene's favourite subject?
2 What is her hobby?
3 What would she like to do when she leaves school?

1 What is Richard's favourite subject?
2 What else does he like doing?
3 What does he sometimes do in the evening?

4 Jutta talks about her schooldays

1 Where did Jutta used to live?
2 What kind of school did she go to?
3 What was the school's main disadvantage?
4 What were her favourite subjects?
5 What is she doing now?

Working in pairs in the following situations you should:
- decide what each of you will say;
- practise the conversation;
- change roles and go through the situation once more.

1 School: 1

You are talking to your German friend about school.

Friend: Asks what time school starts.
You: Say at 9.10 am.
Friend: Asks if you go by bicycle.
You: Say you go by bus.
Friend: Asks what subjects you like.
You: Tell him/her.

2 School: 2

Friend: Asks what kind of school you go to.
You: Tell him/her.
Friend: Asks you to describe your school.
You: Do so.
Friend: Ask what time school finishes.
You: Tell him/her.

3 School: 3

Your penfriend's parents ask you a general question about your school. Prepare an answer saying something about where your school is, its size, how many subjects you study and what you like best.

4 An interview about my school.

Your penfriend has been asked by his/her German teacher to find out information about English schools, so that they can compare the two systems. He/she decides to ask you the nine questions given here. How would you reply?

1. Wieviele Stunden hast du am Tag?
2. Wie lange dauert eine Stunde?
3. Um wieviel Uhr beginnt die Schule?
4. Um wieviel Uhr ist die Schule aus?
5. Wie oft hast du Deutsch?
6. Machst du Biologie?
7. Um wieviel Uhr ist Pause?
8. Trägst du eine Uniform?
9. Gefällt dir die Schule? Warum? / Warum nicht?

5 Interviewing a penfriend

Imagine you've been asked by your German teacher to find out all about the school your penfriend goes to and what he/she likes doing. What questions would you ask? You could use those questions in the last exercise, but you will certainly think of some more. Try them out on other people in your class.

1 My new school

Imagine you have just changed schools after moving house. You haven't time at the moment to send a letter to your penfriend, so you send a postcard instead saying:

a) The new school is very big and modern.

b) You like English best.

c) School starts at 8.45 am and ends at 3.15 pm.

d) You will write soon.

Peter Schmid
OBERWEG 9
6000 FRANKFURT
W. GERMANY

2 My school

Write a letter to your penfriend saying the following things about your school:

1 The kind of school you go to.
2 How many lessons you have each day and how long each one lasts.
3 The name of the headteacher.
4 What you do at lunchtime.

3 A typical day at school

Your penfriend has sent you a letter describing a typical day at his/her school. Write a letter back in which you describe a typical day in your school-week, saying what you like doing best and why.

4 A holiday job

On the recommendation of your penfriend's father, you have been offered a job on a campsite in Germany during the approaching school holidays. As you have not yet met the owner of the campsite, it is suggested that you send him a letter telling him a little about yourself and your studies at school. You should explain how long you have been learning German and what examinations you will be taking.

TOPIC 4: *Holidays and Travel*

You are planning a holiday in Germany with your family and are deciding where to stay.

1 Camping

CAMPINGPLATZ

TARIFE

je Person und Nacht	DM 3,00
je Kind und Nacht (2 - 14 Jahre)	DM 2,00
je Caravan und Nacht	DM 3,50
je Zelt und Nacht	DM 3,00
je kl. Zelt und Nacht	DM 2,00
je Auto und Nacht	DM 1,50
je Krad / Moped und Nacht	DM 0,80
je Fahrrad und Nacht	DM 0,50
Strom je kw/h	DM 0,70

CARAVANVERMIETUNG
mit Vorzelt:
bis 3 Erwachsene oder
2 Erwachsene und 2 Kinder
pro Tag   DM 25,00

Dauerstellplatz   DM 490,-

KINDERSPIELPLATZ - TISCHTENNIS
BOOTSABFAHRT
DUSCHEN UND WASCHMASCHINE
VERKAUFSKIOSK
SAUBERE UND GEPFLEGTE ANLAGEN

Hunde sind erlaubt,
für sie ist eine Gebühr von   DM 1,00
pro Nacht zu entrichten.

Einkaufsmöglichkeiten sind im Ort ausreichend vorhanden.

Eine Anlegestelle für die Personenschiffahrt auf der Mosel befindet sich direkt am Platz.

Geöffnet:
vom 1. April bis 31. Oktober jeden Jahres

1. When is this campsite open?
2. How much is it per person per night?
3. How much would it cost for your ten year-old brother?
4. How much would it cost to hire a caravan?
5. How much do the following cost:
   a a small tent
   b electricity link up?
6. What is there for you and your younger brother to do on this campsite?
7. Your mother wants to know if there are any facilities for washing clothes and where she can do the shopping. What information is given?

2 Hotels and guest houses

Neues Haus, ruhige Lage, direkt am Kurwald, Nähe Schwimmbad, Kurkliniken und Bushaltestelle. Zimmer geschmackvoll eingerichtet mit DU/WC, Minibar, z.T. mit Balkon, alle Zimmer sind mit Telefon ausgestattet. Appartement mit Teeküche. Tischtennis, Solarium, große Liegewiese und Parkplatz. Freundlicher Aufenthaltsraum mit Farbfernseher bietet einen herrlichen Blick ins Moseltal zu den Weinbergen und zur Burg. Gastlichkeit in mosselländischer Atmosphäre. Ganzjährig geöffnet. Bitte Prospekt anfordern.

Haus Carola — Hotel Garni

Das Haus mit der besonderen Note

Bes.: Familie Philipps

Birkenweg 3 / Tel.: 06531 / 8485
5550 Bernkastel-Kues

Part 1

Answer true or false to the following statements about the above hotel.

1 The hotel is open all year round.
2 The hotel has its own swimming pool.
3 All rooms have a telephone.
4 You can play table tennis there.
5 All rooms have a colour TV.

Part 2

1 Your family now wonder about renting a holiday flatlet. To which of these advertisements could you reply?

Pension Haus „Jose"
Fam. Ohlberger
Kapellstraße 52
5590 Cochem-Cond
Tel. 02671/8375

Moderne Ferienwohnung (2-6 Pers.) u. Gästezimmer, alle mit Dusche. Parkplatz. Ruhige Lage. Nähe Freizeitzentrum., Weingut. Sonderangebot Vor- und Nachsaison u. über 14 Tage.

Haus – Pension SONNENSCHEIN

Balkone – Sonnenterrasse –Liegewiese – Sauna – Solarium – Fitneßraum – Grilltisch – Frühstücksbüfett – Fernsicht – Parkplätze ruhige Lage

Klosterstraße 35
5591 Ernst/Mosel
Tel. 02671/7444

Rebenhof

Gästezimmer mit Balkon, Du/Bad-WC, Telefon u. TV-Anschluß
– Frühstücksbüfett –

Brühlstraße 69
5591 Valwig
Tel. 02671/7216

---

2 To which advertisement would you reply if you were looking for somewhere to stay, which offered peace and quiet and something to do indoors should the weather be bad?

3 On holiday in Italy

You receive a letter from your penfriend, who tells you that his/her parents have gone on holiday to Italy. Enclosed with the letter is a copy of the advertisement of the holiday.

> **Super-Reise-Knüller**
>
> **Hotel Ideal, Limone/Gardasee**
>
> Sonderreise vom **nur DM 425.-**
>
> Unsere Super-Leistung: Busreise, 7 Übernachtungen im **4-Sterne-Hotel Ideal**, inkl. reichhaltigem Frühstück und Abendessen (Menuewahl, Salatbuffet). Der **Hotelkomplex Ideal** liegt direkt am Seeufer in einer schönen Gartenanlage. Bars, Tanz-Taverne. Großes Freibad, Hallenbad, Sauna, Solarium, 3 Tennisplätze, Tischtennis und Bocciabahn sorgen für unterhaltsame und sportliche Abwechslung. Alle Zimmer mit Dusche/WC.
>
> Auskunft und Anmeldung unter (02 31) 52 74 36

1. On which date did they set off?
2. How long was the holiday?
3. Where were they staying and what meals were included?
4. What facilities would their room have had?
5. Name any three activities they could have done whilst on holiday.
6. How were they travelling?

4 Youth Hostelling

Youth hostelling is a very popular way of spending a holiday in Germany. Read the article, then answer the questions.

> **Die größte Jugendherberge Europas ...**
>
> ... ist in Frankfurt-Sachsenhausen am "Deutschherrnufer" am Main. Hier gibt es 65 Schlafräume, und 500 Betten. Jeder kann hier fur 13 DM übernachten.
>
> 1987 kamen 80 000 Besucher. Die Hälfte waren Ausländer. Die meisten kommen natürlich im Sommer. Dann muß man rechtzeitig da sein, um noch ein Bett zu bekommen.
>
> Viele Gäste bleiben nur zwei bis drei Tage. Frankfurt ist für die meisten der Start zu einer tollen Europareise.

1. What is special about this particular Youth Hostel?
2. How many dormitories and how many beds are there?
3. How much would it cost to spend a night here?
4. How many of the visitors in 1987 came from abroad?
5. How many nights do the majority of the visitors spend in this Hostel?

5 Information for guests

Whilst staying in your holiday hotel you and your parents see this notice for German guests. Ever eager to demonstrate your knowledge of German you explain to your parents what it all means.

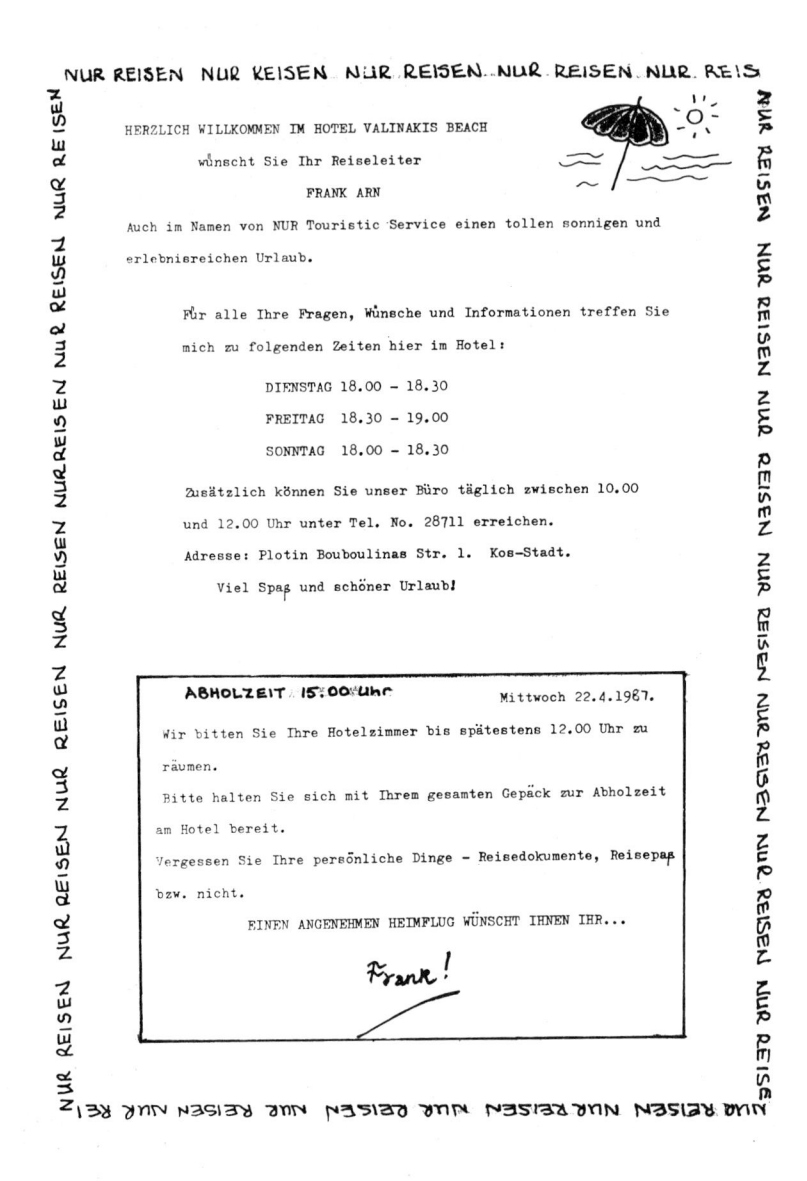

```
HERZLICH WILLKOMMEN IM HOTEL VALINAKIS BEACH
      wünscht Sie Ihr Reiseleiter
              FRANK ARN
Auch im Namen von NUR Touristic Service einen tollen sonnigen und
erlebnisreichen Urlaub.

     Für alle Ihre Fragen, Wünsche und Informationen treffen Sie
     mich zu folgenden Zeiten hier im Hotel:

              DIENSTAG 18.00 - 18.30
              FREITAG   18.30 - 19.00
              SONNTAG   18.00 - 18.30

     Zusätzlich können Sie unser Büro täglich zwischen 10.00
     und 12.00 Uhr unter Tel. No. 28711 erreichen.
     Adresse: Plotin Bouboulinas Str. 1. Kos-Stadt.

          Viel Spaß und schöner Urlaub!
```

```
ABHOLZEIT  15:00 Uhr           Mittwoch 22.4.1987.
Wir bitten Sie Ihre Hotelzimmer bis spätestens 12.00 Uhr zu
räumen.
Bitte halten Sie sich mit Ihrem gesamten Gepäck zur Abholzeit
am Hotel bereit.
Vergessen Sie Ihre persönliche Dinge - Reisedokumente, Reisepaß
bzw. nicht.
     EINEN ANGENEHMEN HEIMFLUG WÜNSCHT IHNEN IHR...

                    Frank!
```

1. On what days and at what times does the NUR REISEN representative visit the hotel?
2. What should guests do who need to speak to him at other times?
3. What does the rep. wish everyone?
4. At what time should guests vacate their rooms?
5. What time will they be picked up to go home?
6. What things should they not forget?
7. What does he finally wish everyone?

6 Visit the Süd-Eiffel

This article is taken from a brochure inviting people to spend their holidays in the Süd-Eiffel area of Germany.

> Zu jeder Jahreszeit garantieren das Kylltal sowie die beiden Naturparks an der deutsch-luxemburgischen und -belgischen Grenze Erholung und Entspannung.
>
> **Zwei NATURPARKS - ein FERIENKREIS - SÜD-EIFEL**
>
> Die Süd-Eifel um Bitburg und um Prüm mit den vielfältigen Möglichkeiten, wo Kraft und Gesundheit getankt wird, bietet Urlaub und Ferien nach Maß.
>
> Kuren, Wandern, Reiten, Tennis, Schwimmen, Angeln, Wassersport, Hobby-Geologie sowie Archäologie und Ski - besonders geeignet für Langlauf - sind nur eine kleine Auswahl aus dem umfangreichen Programm.
>
> Hotels, Pensionen, Feriendörfer, Bauernhöfe und Privatvermieter freuen sich auf „IHREN" Besuch.
>
> Individuelle Gastlichkeit mit Speisen aus feinster Küche und Ursprünglichkeit abseits vom Massentourismus ist das besondere Flair, das die Süd-Eifel auszeichnet.
>
> Und dann das milde Klima in Höhen von 160 - 180 m NN sowie das gesundheitsfördernde Mittelgebirgsklima in Höhenlagen bis 700 m NN, geben diesem Ferienkreis einen hohen heilklimatischen Erholungswert.

Answer true or false to these items.

1 This area of Germany is near the German/Italian border.
2 You could go riding here.
3 There is a very good campsite here.
4 It is very cold in winter and very hot in summer.

7 A visit to Trier

Whilst staying in Germany, you decide to go on an organized coach trip to the city of Trier. You obtain a leaflet about it from the travel agent. You are staying in Bernkastel-Kues.

DONNERSTAG

TRIER: zur ältesten Stadt Deutschlands.

Hinfahrt durch das Moseltal über Neumagen. In Trier Stadtrundfahrt zu den bekannten Sehenswürdigkeiten wie: Amphitheater, Kaiserthermen, römische Basilika, Porta Nigra, Paulinskirche u.v.m.
Anschließend Kaffeepause und Möglichkeit zum Besuch weiterer Sehenswürdigkeiten in der Römerstadt Trier. 18.30 Uhr Rückfahrt durch die Vordereifel. Rückankunft gegen 19.30 Uhr.

Fahrpreis: Erwachsene 13,-- DM
Kinder 8,-- DM

Zusteigemöglichkeiten:

13.10 Uhr Ürzig — Denkmal
13.15 Uhr Zeltingen — Waage
13.20 Uhr Wehlen — Brücke Graach
13.25 Uhr Graach — Bushaltestelle
13.30 Uhr Bernkastel-Kues — Bundesbahnhof
13.35 Uhr Lieser — Bushaltestelle
13.40 Uhr Mülheim — Apotheke

1. What time does the coach leave from Bernkastel-Kues?
2. Where exactly does it leave from in Bernkastel?
3. How much will it cost for you?
4. When does the coach leave Trier and about what time will you get back?
5. The tour includes a Stadtrundfahrt — what do you think this is?

8 Room to let

This photograph was taken outside a Gasthaus in Bernkastel.

1. What is the price of the room per person?
2. What facilities does the room have?
3. Is breakfast extra?
4. What two added attractions are there?

9 A letter from Germany

In this letter, Brigitte talks about how she and her family spent the Easter holidays.

1. How long has the writer now been back at her job in a school?
2. Where has she been on holiday?
3. What does she say about the weather?
4. What did Klaus do during the holidays?
5. Why does she mention Crete?
6. What was the weather like in February?
7. What is the weather in Lüdenscheid like at the time of writing?

Lüdenscheid 1. Mai 1987

Lieber Dave, Liebe Jen,

Nach den Osterferien, die wir ganz besonders stark herbeigesehnt hatten, sind wir schon wieder eine Woche in der Schule gewesen, und der Alltagsbetrieb hat uns längst wieder.

Unser Urlaub in Italien war wunderschön, auch wenn das Wetter — untypischerweise — nicht so beständig war, wie sonst um diese Zeit. Trotzdem haben wir natürlich am Strand sein können, und Klaus hat mehrmals gebadet.

Ob bei Eurer Ankunft auf Kreta aller Schnee geschmolzen war? Bis kurz vor Beginn der Ferien war dort ja wohl noch tiefster

Winter. Auch wir bekamen nach Eurer Abreise von hier im Februar noch mehrfach Unmengen von Schnee und haben uns deshalb besonders stark auf die Sonne im Süden gefreut. Auch hier waren die Temperaturen in den letzten Tagen ungewöhnlich hoch, so daß wir die in Italien erlangte Bräune ein wenig kultivieren konnten.
Herzliche Grüße, auch an Eure Familie und alle Bekannten in Leeds.
Deine,
Brigitte.

10 Holiday weather

Das Wetter
Quelle: Wetteramt Essen

Sonnig und warm
Wetterlage
Ein Hoch über Mitteleuropa bestimmt das Wetter in Deutschland.
Vorhersage für heute
Überwiegend heiter und durchweg trocken. Anstieg der Temperaturen bis 18 Grad, nachts um 8 Grad. Schwacher Südostwind.
Weitere Aussichten
Sonnig und noch weiter ansteigende Temperaturen.
Reisewetter
Südfrankreich: Heiter bis wolkig, 19 bis 24 Grad.
Spanien: Noch heiter, 24 Grad.
Österreich, Schweiz: Meist sonnig, im Westen später aufkommende Schauer und Gewitter. Temperatur auf 18 bis 26 Grad ansteigend, in 2000 m bis 12 Grad.

1 What was the weather forecast for Germany?
2 What was the forecast for the following countries:
  a the South of France
  b Spain
  c Austria and Switzerland?

11 Europe by rail

Buying a card like this entitles a family to certain reductions on rail tickets.

RAIL EUROP F

CIV 80 Gültig 1 Jahr DB

vom 12 05 85 bis 11 05 86

Die ausstellende Bahn bestätigt die Rechtmäßigkeit der Eintragungen.

Tagesstempel der Ausgabestelle

Deutsche Bundesbahn
Düsseldorf Hbf
1 1. 05. 1985
400   081257

Nr. 000000 DM 20,-

1 How long is the card valid for?
2 Where was this card issued?
3 How much did it cost?

1 Last year's holidays

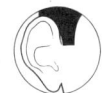

Four German teenagers are talking about their summer holidays last year.

A Anja

1. Where did she spend her holidays?
2. Where was the hotel situated?
3. What criticism does she make of the resort?

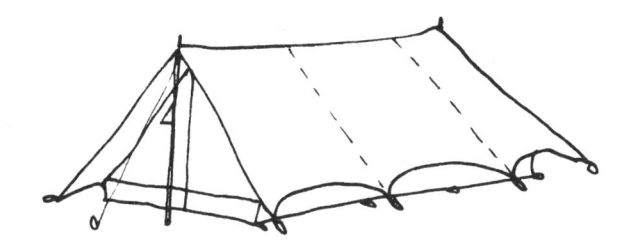

B Kurt

1. How long did Kurt spend camping?
2. Name two activities in which he took part at the campsite.

C Heike

1. When did Heike fly to the States?
2. With whom did she stay?
3. She mentions a sauna at the place where she stayed. Name two other facilities.

D Arne

1. Where did Arne spend his holidays?
2. What did he do?
3. Why is he saving his pocket money?

2 Holiday preferences

Three German people were asked what kind of holiday they preferred — *camping, youth hostelling,* or *staying in hotels.*

- A 1 What does this person like doing?
-    2 What reasons does she give?
- B 1 What, for this person, are the advantages of youth hostelling?
- C 1 This person likes to stay in hotels. Why?

3 Barbara remembers her holidays

1 Where did Barbara go on her holidays?
2 Where did she stay?
3 How did she get there?
4 What was the weather like during her stay?
5 What did she do there?

4 Weather forecast

Whilst on holiday in Germany you hear this weather forecast. Can you fill in this table?

Area	General outlook	Highest temperatures
North		27–30°C
West	Cloudy	
South		

What does the announcer say about the weather for the coming weekend?

1 Booking a room in an hotel

You have arrived at an hotel in Germany and want to book a room.

1. Ask if they have any rooms free.
2. Say you would like a single room with a shower for you and a double room with a bath for your parents.
3. Ask what time breakfast is.

2 At the Youth Hostel

On your arrival in Germany you telephone the Youth Hostel to see if there is room for you and a friend.

1. Ask if they still have some beds free.
2. Say you would like two for the night.
3. Ask what it costs.

3 Where do you go on holiday?

You are talking about holidays with your penfriend's mother. She asks where you usually spend your holidays and how you get there. She also asks how long you stay.

1. Say you go to the coast.
2. Say you usually go by car.
3. Say you usually stay two weeks.

4 Last year's holiday

You are talking with a penfriend.

1. Ask where he/she spent the summer holidays last year.
2. Ask what the weather was like.
3. Ask what he/she did in the evening.

5 An excursion

You want to go on a day excursion to Bonn. You go to the local travel agent to find out about trips.

1. Ask what time the coach leaves.
2. Ask how much it costs.
3. Ask if that trip includes lunch.

6 At the campsite

You arrive at a campsite, but unfortunately it is full.

1. Ask the owner if there is another campsite nearby.
2. Ask the best way to get there.
3. Ask if you can telephone from his office.

In the following situations you have to work out for yourself what to say in German.

7 Finding somewhere to stay

You are with another English person touring Germany on a shoe-string budget. You have a maximum of 15 DM to spend per night on somewhere to stay and you know that there is no Youth Hostel in the town. You go to the Verkehrsamt where you explain your situation and ask for help in finding somewhere to stay.

8 Working on a campsite

You have been camping with your family for two weeks in the Black Forest and have helped the proprietor in the campsite's shop at busy times. You (and your parents) think that your German would benefit if you were to stay on there, continuing to help and improving your accent. You go to the owner and explain what you have in mind. Say your German is getting better everyday and that you can also speak some French. Say that you like the area and that you will work hard.

9 Travelling to Munich

You have been spending a few days in Frankfurt and want to move south to Munich. You have been expressly forbidden by your parents to hitch-hike; you don't like travelling at night and you don't want to spend a fortune on fares. You go to the Tourist Office and enquire about the cheapest way of getting to Munich. When you have done so, ask where the nearest travel agent is, so you can book a ticket.

10 Youth Hostel booking

You arrive with two friends in Germany and go to the Youth Hostel where you have made a booking by letter some three weeks previously. The warden can find no trace of your booking. Be prepared to give your name and address, details of the booking — number of beds for how many nights — and find out the cost of your stay.

11 A complaint

You have just spent a night on a campsite with your parents and are most disappointed with the facilities. You go to the owner to complain that the toilets are dirty, the hot showers are cold and you had to wait until 10 am for the shop to open. Say you are leaving and would like your money back.

12 Holiday interview

Your teacher is bringing a German person to your lesson to help you with the topic of holidays. You are going to interview him about his holidays last year. Think of all the questions you could ask him and try them out with a partner, taking it in turns to be the German person.

13 My holidays (a short talk)

You have been asked to give a short talk in German on your holidays. Work out what you could say — remember to mention dates, travel, weather and the things you did.

1 A postcard

You are on holiday by the sea in England. Write a postcard in German to your penfriend, saying the following things:

a. The hotel is small but nice.
b. The weather is warm.
c. You go swimming everyday.

Peter Schmid
OBERWEG 9
6000 FRANKFURT
W. GERMANY

2 A telephone message

Your penfriend's grandmother has gone away on holiday. You are alone in the house in Germany when she rings to say she has arrived safely. Take a message for the family saying:

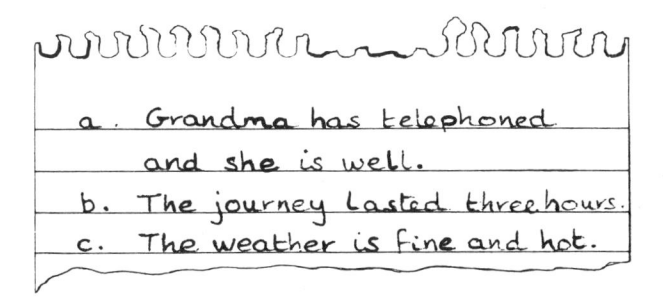

a. Grandma has telephoned and she is well.
b. The journey lasted three hours.
c. The weather is fine and hot.

3 Letter to a Youth Hostel: 1

Write a short letter to the Youth Hostel in Bonn saying you are visiting Germany in the summer and would like to know the cost of an overnight stay and also if you can hire a sleeping bag. Ask what time the Youth Hostel closes at night and if it is near the station.

4 Letter to a Youth Hostel: 2

You receive an answer to the above letter and decide to make a booking. Say you would like to reserve two beds from 12 to 15 August inclusive and would like to hire one sleeping bag. Say you will be arriving at about 10 pm.

5 A booking form

You have written to an hotel in Germany about the possibility of making a booking. You have received a reply asking you to fill in the enclosed form. You wish to book the following:

1. One double room with a shower, with a view of the mountains.
2. One double room with a balcony.
3. One extra bed.

The booking is for four adults and one child from the 6 to 13 June. Fill in the form accordingly and sign and date it in the appropriate places.

Reservieren Sie für:

Name: _____

Strasse: _____

PLZ, Wohnort: _____

Telefon: _____   _____

_____ Doppelzimmer mit Dusche, Balkon, Seeseite

_____ Doppelzimmer mit Dusche, ohne Balkon, Bergseite

_____ Studio mit Bad, Balkon, Seeseite

_____ Zusatzbett(en)

_____ Anzahl Erwachsene   _____ Anzahl Kinder

Anreisetag: _____   Abreisetag: _____

                                        Unterschrift:

Datum: _____   _____

6 A letter to an hotel

You have been helping a neighbour to book a room in an hotel in Interlaken, Switzerland. You have already written one letter asking about the cost and have received this reply. Your neighbour asks you to write back on her behalf saying:

1. You would like to book a double room with breakfast for two people from 26 July to 5 August.
2. You will be arriving by train at about 2 pm.
3. Ask them to send a town plan so that you can find your way from the station to the hotel.

```
HOTEL EINTRACHT
Seni & Marc Giger
Rosenstrasse 17
3800 INTERLAKEN
Tel. 036 22 32 25
                                    Frau S. Fraser
                                    4 Longmeadow

                                    Batley
                                    West Yorks

                                    England

                        Interlaken, den 1. Febr.


Sehr geehrte Frau Fraser.

Ich habe heute Ihren Brief erhalten und teile Ihnen gerne
Unsere Konditionen mit.

Ein Doppelzimmer mit Frühstück für zwei Personen kostet
                Fr. 60.-.

Beiliegend sende ich Ihnen noch eine POstkarte von unserem
Hotel.

Es würde uns sehr freuen, Sie als Gast bei uns begrüssen
zu dürfen, und sende Ihnen unsere

                            allerbesten Grüsse.
```

7 A forthcoming visit

Write a letter to your penfriend about your forthcoming visit. Include the following information:

1. The exact dates of your visit.
2. You will be travelling by plane.
3. The time of your arrival.
4. Ask if he can meet you at the airport.

TOPIC 5: *Travel and Transport*

1 Travelling in Germany

A

A 1 How much was this ticket?
2 Was it for a child or an adult?
3 How many journeys was it valid for?

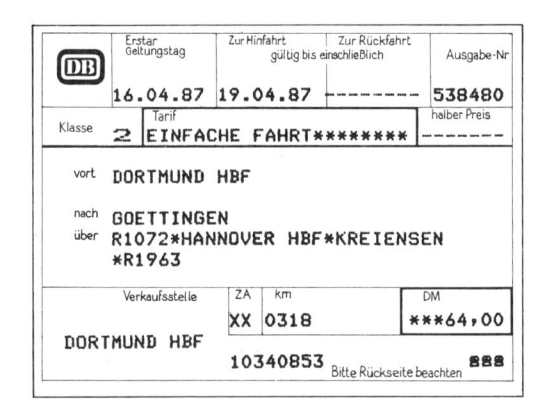

B

B 1 This ticket was bought in Dortmund — where was the traveller going?
2 How much did it cost?
3 Was it for a single or a return journey?
4 What class of ticket is it?
5 How long in kilometres was the journey?

C

C 1 This ticket records that the person paid a *Zuschlag* — what is this?
2 How much was the *Zuschlag*?

46

2 Travelling by aeroplane

Your penfriend is coming to visit you and is flying from Düsseldorf to Manchester. He/she has sent you the timetable and tells you that he/she will be taking the first flight from Düsseldorf to Manchester on Tuesday 14 July. He/she asks if you will meet him/her at the airport in Manchester.

1 What time is his/her flight due to arrive?
2 What flight number will you have to look for?

DÜSSELDORF → MANCHESTER

ABFLUG / DEPARTURE

Flug-steig	Flug	Mo	Di	Mi	Do	Fr	Sa	So	nach/to an/ar
A	AZ 417	08.00	08.00	08.00	08.00	08.00	08.00	08.00	Mailand 09.25
A	LH 276	09.35	09.35	09.35	09.35	09.35	09.35	09.35	11.00
A	AZ 449	17.10	17.10	17.10	17.10	17.10	17.10	17.10	18.35
A	LH 278	20.50	20.50	20.50	20.50	20.50	—	20.50	22.15
A	LH 188	—	—	—	—	—	10.40	—	Malaga 13.40
A	LH 076	09.20	09.20	09.20	09.20	09.20	—	09.20	Manchester 09.50
B	BA 925	—	—	—	—	—	11.30	—	12.35
B	BA 953	19.40	19.40	19.40	19.40	19.40	—	19.40	20.05
A	LH 434	—	—	—	12.05	—	—	12.05	Miami 16.15
B	AC 865	12.05	12.05	—	—	12.05	12.05	12.05	Montreal 15.50
A	SU 202	—	—	—	—	—	12.40	—	Moskau 17.55
A	LH 978	06.50	06.50	06.50	06.50	06.50	—	—	München 07.55
A	LH 941	07.30	—	—	—	—	—	—	08.35
A	LH 292	07.50	07.50	07.50	07.50	07.50	07.50	07.50	08.55
A	LH 358	08.50	08.50	08.50	08.50	08.50	08.50	08.50	09.55
A	LH 979	09.50	09.50	09.50	09.50	09.50	—	—	10.55
A	LH 362	11.50	11.50	11.50	11.50	11.50	11.50	11.50	12.55
A	LH 316	12.50	12.50	12.50	12.50	12.50	12.50	12.50	13.55
A	LH 302	13.50	13.50	13.50	13.50	13.50	13.50	13.50	14.55
A	LH 980	14.50	14.50	14.50	14.50	14.50	—	—	15.55
A	LH 981	16.50	16.50	16.50	16.50	16.50	16.50	16.50	17.55
A	LH 328	17.50	17.50	17.50	17.50	17.50	17.50	17.50	18.55
A	LH 982	19.50	19.50	19.50	19.50	19.50	—	19.50	20.55
A	LH 021	20.50	20.50	20.50	20.50	20.50	20.50	20.50	21.50

He/she plans to return home on a Sunday.

1 What time will his/her return flight leave Manchester?
2 What time will the plane land in Düsseldorf?

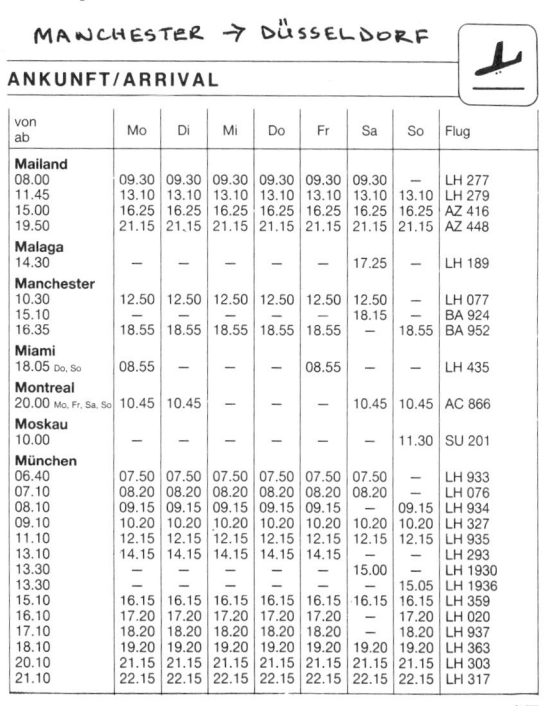

MANCHESTER → DÜSSELDORF

ANKUNFT / ARRIVAL

von ab	Mo	Di	Mi	Do	Fr	Sa	So	Flug
Mailand								
08.00	09.30	09.30	09.30	09.30	09.30	09.30	—	LH 277
11.45	13.10	13.10	13.10	13.10	13.10	13.10	13.10	LH 279
15.00	16.25	16.25	16.25	16.25	16.25	16.25	16.25	AZ 416
19.50	21.15	21.15	21.15	21.15	21.15	21.15	21.15	AZ 448
Malaga								
14.30	—	—	—	—	—	17.25	—	LH 189
Manchester								
10.30	12.50	12.50	12.50	12.50	12.50	12.50	—	LH 077
15.10	—	—	—	—	—	18.15	—	BA 924
16.35	18.55	18.55	18.55	18.55	18.55	—	18.55	BA 952
Miami								
18.05 Do, So	08.55	—	—	08.55	—	—	—	LH 435
Montreal								
20.00 Mo, Fr, Sa, So	10.45	10.45	—	—	10.45	10.45	10.45	AC 866
Moskau								
10.00	—	—	—	—	—	11.30	—	SU 201
München								
06.40	07.50	07.50	07.50	07.50	07.50	07.50	—	LH 933
07.10	08.20	08.20	08.20	08.20	08.20	08.20	—	LH 076
08.10	09.15	09.15	09.15	09.15	09.15	—	09.15	LH 934
09.10	10.20	10.20	10.20	10.20	10.20	10.20	10.20	LH 327
11.10	12.15	12.15	12.15	12.15	12.15	12.15	12.15	LH 935
13.10	14.15	14.15	14.15	14.15	14.15	—	—	LH 293
13.30	—	—	—	—	—	15.00	—	LH 1930
13.30	—	—	—	—	—	—	15.05	LH 1936
15.10	16.15	16.15	16.15	16.15	16.15	16.15	16.15	LH 359
16.10	17.20	17.20	17.20	17.20	17.20	—	17.20	LH 020
17.10	18.20	18.20	18.20	18.20	18.20	—	18.20	LH 937
18.10	19.20	19.20	19.20	19.20	19.20	—	19.20	LH 363
20.10	21.15	21.15	21.15	21.15	21.15	21.15	21.15	LH 303
21.10	22.15	22.15	22.15	22.15	22.15	22.15	22.15	LH 317

47

3 Cycling

You and your penfriend receive an invitation to spend a few days with a relative in another part of Germany. You'd like to have the chance to do some cycling, but it is too far to actually go to this relative's house by bike. Your penfriend's father comes up with two possible solutions and suggests you read this leaflet.

What are the two solutions?

Ihr Fahrrad kommt genauso zügig an wie Sie.

Wenn Sie mit der Bahn auf Urlaubsreise gehen, brauchen Sie selbstverständlich nicht auf Ihr Fahrrad zu verzichten. Geben Sie es einfach vor der Abreise zusammen mit Ihren Koffern rechtzeitig auf. Die Bahn fährt es dann im Gepäckwagen bis an Ihr Urlaubsziel.

Und sobald Sie angekommen sind, können Sie Ihr Rad bei der Gepäckabfertigung abholen.

An vielen Bahnhöfen können Sie auch ein Fahrrad leihen, wenn Sie möchten. Über das „Wo" und „Wie" informiert Sie eine spezielle Broschüre, die Sie an jeder Gepäckabfertigung bekommen.

4 Road safety: 1

In a letter to your penfriend you have asked about how old you have to be to drive a car in Germany. In his/her reply he/she has enclosed this information. Answer true or false to the following questions.

1 You have to be 18 to drive a car.
2 At 16 you can ride a moped.
3 You have to take a test on the Highway Code before you can ride off on your motorised cycle (*Mofa*).
4 In Germany you need a licence to ride a bicycle.

Verkehrssicherheit

Wer ein **Auto** oder ein **schweres Motorrad** fahren will, muß eine Fahrschule besuchen und kann frühestens **mit 18 Jahren** nach einer **Prüfung** die **Fahrerlaubnis** erhalten.

Ein **Leichtkraftrad** oder **Moped** kann man schon **mit 16 Jahren** benutzen, aber nur, wenn man einen **Führerschein** erworben hat. Wenn Du **15 Jahre** alt bist, darfst Du mit einem **Mofa** fahren; aber vorher mußt Du seit dem 1. April 1980 in einer **Prüfung** nachweisen, daß Du die **Verkehrszeichen** und **Gefahrensituationen** kennst.

Und mit dem **Fahrrad** kannst Du **sofort** losfahren . . .

Halt! So einfach ist es nicht!

Du fährst als ungeschützter Radfahrer, der leicht übersehen wird, auf der gleichen belebten Straße wie alle anderen Verkehrsteilnehmer. Aber bist Du Dir auch voll bewußt, welchen Gefahren Du Dich aussetzen wirst und welche Gefahr Du auch für andere bedeuten kannst?

5 Road safety: 2

Look carefully at this photograph.

1 What is being offered here and to whom?
2 How much does the service cost?
3 What must you have with you?

OPTIK FUHR

Amtlicher SEHTEST für Führerscheinbewerber

Gebühr DM 5,70
Personalausweis erforderlich

6 At the petrol station

1 What kind of petrol is being advertised here?
2 When will you be able to buy this petrol?

NEU BEI UNS

ab sofort können Sie an unserer Tankstelle auch **bleifreies Benzin** tanken.

Freie Tankstelle

Adele Felser

Hauptstraße 66
5591 Gevenich
Telefon 0 26 78 / 8 11

7 Sightseeing

A 1 What can you hire here?
   2 How long do you get for the price given?
   3 How much would it cost for two people?
   4 How much would it cost for five people?
   5 How old do you have to be to hire this transport?
   6 Do you need a licence?

B This photograph is of an advertisement for a boat trip on the Mosel river. Are these statements true or false?

   1 There are six trips per day.
   2 Each trip lasts for one hour.
   3 It costs 6 DM for adults.
   4 There is a shorter trip also on offer.

C This photograph shows details of another boat journey.
1. Where is this boat trip going to?
2. What two things can you get at the kiosk?
3. Can you explain the difference between a *Rundfahrt*, as advertised in the previous photograph, and the trip advertised here?

SCHIFFSFAHRTEN
Täglich nach BEILSTEIN
mit Schleusendurchfahrt
Aufenthalt und zurück

Abfahrt: 10³⁰ 13¹⁵ 14³⁰ 16⁰⁰ h
Rückkunft ca. 12⁵⁰ 15²⁰ 17⁵⁰ 17⁵⁰ h
Auskunft und Fahrscheine
hier am Kiosk
MOSELPERSONENSCHIFFAHRT
Gebr. Kolb · 5591 Briedern
☎ 02673 / 1515

8 Inter-Rail

Your penfriend writes to tell you about his/her holiday plans. With his/her older brother and a group of friends, he/she is planning to tour Europe using an Inter-Rail pass. He/she sends you some information about how he/she is going to go about it.

1. What age limits are there on this ticket?
2. How much will your penfriend have to pay?
3. How long is the ticket valid for?
4. How do you get a ticket like this?
5. Where do German Railways recommend travellers stay?
6. What facilities do German Railways provide for changing money?

INTER-RAIL
Für alle unter 23.
Einen Monat durch 21 Länder für 350,- DM.
Tips für Trips mit Inter-Rail.

Wo Sie die Inter-Rail-Karte erhalten.

Bei allen Fahrkartenschaltern, DER-Reisebüros oder anderen DB-Verkaufsagenturen. Beim Kauf einfach den Personalausweis oder Reisepaß vorlegen, ein Formular ausfüllen und die Inter-Rail-Karte mitnehmen. Für ganze 350 Mark.

Wo man unterwegs preisgünstig übernachten kann.

Am preiswertesten kommt man in Jugendherbergen unter. Für die Unterkunft benötigen Sie beinahe immer einen internationalen Ausweis, der vom Verband der „International Youth Hostel Federation" anerkannt wird.

Wo man Finanzielles regeln kann.

In vielen Bahnhöfen der Deutschen Bundesbahn gibt es Wechselstuben der „Deutschen Verkehrs-Kredit-Bank AG (DVKB)". Die DVKB wechselt Ihr Geld in die Währungen aller Länder, in denen Ihre Inter-Rail-Karte gilt.

1 Trains ...

A You are with your penfriend at the station, finding out about trains to Frankfurt. Listen to the conversation between your penfriend and the man in the ticket office.

1. When does the first train leave?
2. Why doesn't your penfriend want to take this train?
3. What does a return ticket cost?
4. What additional charge is there?
5. How long will the journey take?

B Whilst waiting at the station you hear these announcements.

1. How late is this train?
2. What time does the train leave for Vienna and from which platform?
3. How much time is there before the train to Düsseldorf departs and from which platform will it leave?

2 ... and Planes

You hear these announcements whilst you are waiting at the airport.

1. To which gate are passengers being asked to go?
2. Where does the announcer ask Herr Schmid to go?

3 Getting to school

These schoolchildren were asked how they go to school each day and how long their journey lasts. Complete the table when you have listened to the tape.

	Transport	Time
1		
2		
3		
4		

4 Vera's journey to England

A German student describes her journey to the north of England.

1. How did she get to Aachen?
2. Who was with her at this point?
3. Where did she stay overnight?
4. Which ferry did she travel on to England?
5. Why did she not go to the disco on the ferry?
6. What happened to her when she arrived in Hull?

1 At the station

Could you ask the following questions?

1 The price of a return ticket to Hamburg.
2 The time of the next train to Hamburg.
3 The arrival time of the train in Hamburg.
4 Which platform the train leaves from.
5 If passengers for Hamburg have to change.

2 Going to Düsseldorf

You want to go to Düsseldorf. With a partner, practise what you would say.

Traveller	Ticket clerk
A second class ticket to Düsseldorf, please.	Single or return?
A return. What does it cost?	55 DM
When does it leave and from which platform?	16.10 Platform 3.
When does the train arrive?	17.05

Now change roles

You can vary this conversation by asking for a single first class ticket and also by changing the platform number and train times. Using the conversation printed above to help you, make up another one with your partner.

3 Going to Cologne

You are on your way to see your friend by train. The person sitting next to you wants to know about the journey.

Person: Says 'excuse me' and asks whether the train goes direct to Cologne.
You: Say he/she must change trains.
Person: Asks where.
You: Say in Kassel.
Person: Asks how much longer to Kassel.
You: Say about 25 minutes.

4 Taking the tram

You are in the town and want to visit a museum. You ask a passer-by the best way to get there and she suggests by tram.

Find out which tram you should take, where the nearest stop is and where you should get off.

5 Getting to school

With your partner, find out how you each get to school and how long your journey takes. Find out what time you each leave the house in the morning.

6 Standing room only

The train you are travelling on in Germany is very full and so far you have been unable to find a seat in a second class carriage. You are very tired and find a first class carriage which is empty. You get comfortable when along comes the inspector.

Inspector: Tells you to move back to second class.
You: Explain why you are sitting there and that you are very tired.
Inspector: Tells you that you can stay if you pay a supplement.
You: Ask how much the supplement is and when he tells you, agree to pay.

7 At the petrol station: 1

You are with your parents holidaying by car in Germany. You stop for petrol in a small village.

You: Ask for the car to be filled up.
Attendant: Asks what kind of petrol you would like.
You: Say normal.
Attendant: Asks if he should check the tyres.
You: Say no thanks, but ask him to check the oil.

8 At the petrol station: 2

You: Ask for 20 DM of super.
Ask if you can buy a map there.
Ask the attendant to check the water.

9 Breakdown

You have broken down on the motorway not far from Munich. You go to the nearest emergency telephone. Explain to the person at the other end of the telephone what has happened. Say you are on the motorway travelling south, telephone 27. You are travelling in a white, English Ford Fiesta and ask how long you will have to wait.

10 Repairs

Your father pulls in at a garage repair shop the day before you are due to set off home to England. You explain to the mechanic that the car brakes are faulty. He wants to know how long they have been faulty and you tell him since yesterday. He suggests you leave the car with him while he checks it over and asks you to come back tomorrow. Say that is impossible and explain why. Ask if he could check the car now.

1 Arrival times

You have received a letter from your penfriend, confirming that he/she is expecting a visit from you shortly. Send him/her a postcard with the brief details of your visit.

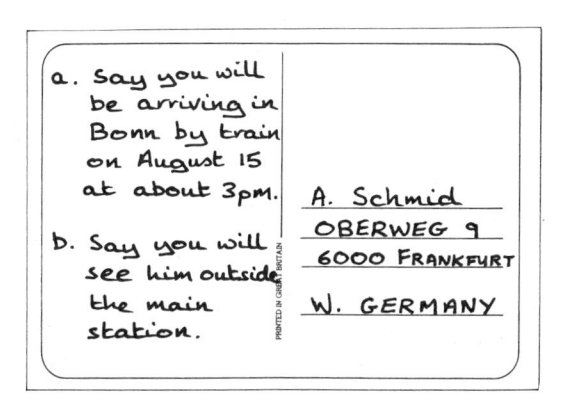

a. Say you will be arriving in Bonn by train on August 15 at about 3pm.

b. Say you will see him outside the main station.

A. Schmid
OBERWEG 9
6000 FRANKFURT
W. GERMANY

2 Which bus?

Your penfriend is staying with you and whilst you have to go to school he/she decides to go into town for a look round. He/she asks you to jot down the number of the bus he/she should take, what time the bus leaves and where the bus stop is. Tell him/her what time the bus leaves town and how much it costs.

3 Breakdown message

You are travelling in Germany by car and have a breakdown. There is no telephone nearby, but a kind motorist stops and asks if he can help. You ask him to telephone a garage when he gets to the next town. He agrees to do so, but asks you to write down the information for him in German so that he won't forget.
   Write down your name, where you are, what you think is wrong with the car and a brief description of the car.

4 Visiting a penfriend

Write a short letter to your penfriend thanking him/her for his/her invitation to stay. Say you will be travelling on 20 July, by plane from Heathrow. Tell him/her what time the plane leaves and what time it should arrive. Ask him/her to meet you at the airport if possible.

5 A new car

Write a letter to a friend in Germany about the new car your big sister has just bought. Say you have been to the coast in it and that you would like to have a car when you are old enough. Ask how old you have to be to drive in Germany.

6 An accident

You have recently returned to England after spending a holiday in Germany. Whilst there you witnessed the accident your penfriend's brother had on his bicycle in the village. The German police have written to you asking for your account of what happened. Write your report.

7 A day out in the car

Using the series of pictures as a guide, write to your penfriend telling him/her what happened to you, and your family, when you went out in the car last weekend.

TOPIC 6: *Free Time and Entertainment*

1 Tickets

A

1 What was this an entry ticket for?
2 How much did it cost?

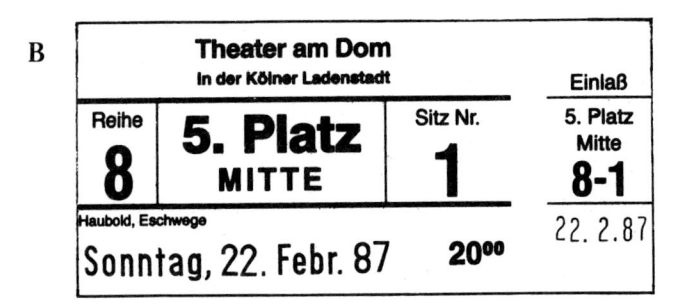

B

1 What was this ticket for?
2 What row was the seat on?
3 What day and what date was it valid for?
4 What time did the performance begin?

C This is a receipt for the entrance fee paid by a school group to the Planetarium in Bochum.

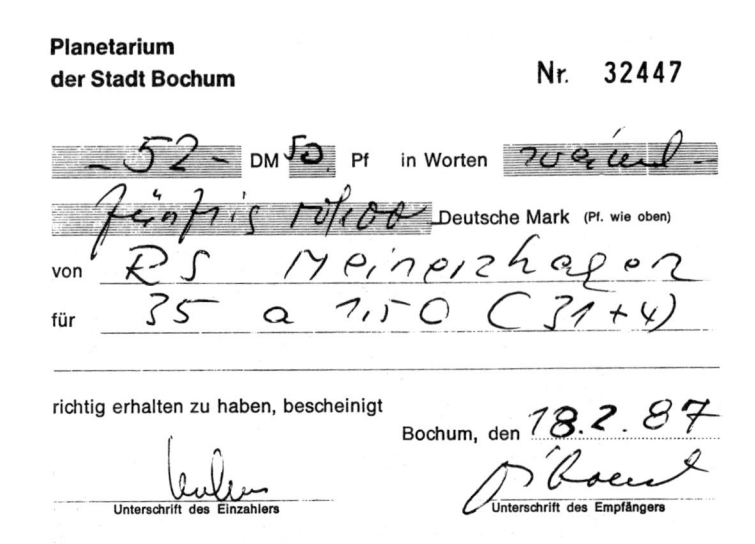

1 How much did it cost to go in?
2 How many people went in?

D This is a receipt for a visit to some caves.
1 How much did it cost per child?
2 How much did it cost for the adults in the party?

Tropfsteinhöhle Attendorn

5952 Attendorn · Postfach 104 · Fernsprecher 02722/2400

Besichtigung   Nr.   3969

Schulkinder ...... 31 ...... á 2.50 = DM 77.50

Aufsichtspersonen 2   frei

Begleitpersonen ...... / ...... á / = DM /

einschl. 14 % Mwst.   Summe = DM 77.50

Attendorn, 16/02/87   Betrag erhalten:

2 Wildlife Park

1 How much does it cost to get into the park for:
   a children?
   b adults?
2 How many animals are there?
3 What is there especially for children?

Bärenstark: Wildpark Lüneburger Heide
500 Tiere
Direkt vor Ihrer Haustür
Restaurant · Kinderspielplätze
Eintritt nur:
Erwachs. 6,- DM
Kinder 4,- DM
2116 HANSTEDT-NINDORF
Tel. 04184-1041
Nahe Heidezentrum Hanstedt-Undeloh-Wilsede

3 A concert

Mittwoch 10. 9. 20.00

REINHARD MEY *live*

Endlich wieder auf Tournee

Eintritt: ab 15.- DM

1. When could you see Reinhard May?
2. How much would the cheapest seats be?

4 A party

> **Pfingst-Sonntag**
> **18. 5.**
> ab 19.00
>
> Große
>
> # TANZ-PARTY
>
> Eintritt: 10.- DM

1. What kind of party is advertised here?
2. What date is the party on?
3. What time does the party start?
4. How much does it cost to get in?

5 Disco

1. What date is the disco on?
2. Why do you think there are three exclamation marks after the time?
3. How much does it cost to get in?
4. What are the prizes in the raffle?
5. What could you buy to drink there?

6 Keeping fit

1 What activity is advertised here?
2 When should you meet if you want to take part?
3 Why might you need to contact Walter Büchel?

Lauf Treff

Treffpunkt

Jeden Mittwoch um 19 Uhr
(von April bis September)
am Haupteingang des
Feriendorfs der Bundespost
in Prüm.

Auskunft:
Walter Büchel, Tel. 06551/2265
Prüm, Pfannstr. 3

Laufen Sie mit!

Ski-Klub Prüm

7 What to do in your free-time

FREIZEITEINRICHTUNGEN

Freizeitzentrum Cochem-Cond

Freibad:	täglich	von 08.00 - 20.00 Uhr	3,50 Erwachsene	2,00 Jugendliche	1,00 Gruppen
Hallenbad:			Kurzzeittarife: Einzelkarte		
Mo		von 14.00 - 22.00 Uhr	6,00 Erw.	4,00 Jugendl.	3,00 Kinder 2,50 Gruppen
Di, Mi, Do		von 08.00 - 22.00 Uhr	Langzeittarife: Einzelkarte		
Freitag „Warmbadetag"		von 10.00 - 22.00 Uhr	10,00 Erw.	6,00 Jugendl.	4,00 Kinder
Sa, So, Feiertag		von 10.00 - 19.00 Uhr	Zeitkarte: 50,- DM	240 Punktekarte: 120,- DM	
Sauna:	Mo - Fr	von 14.00 - 22.00 Uhr	Einzelkarte		
	Sa - So	von 10.00 - 19.00 Uhr	14,00 Erw.	10,00 Jugendliche	7,00 Kinder
Minigolf:	täglich	von 10.00 - 20.00 Uhr	2,50 Erw.		2,00 Kinder
Tennis:	Mo - Fr	von 08.00 - 15.00 Uhr	Platz 12,50 DM stdl. - Karten an der Schwimmbadkasse		

Look at the notice above and answer true or false to these statements.

1. The outdoor swimming pool opens at 8 am.
2. It costs 3,50 DM for a young person to get into the pool.
3. The indoor pool opens at 8 am at weekends.
4. It closes at 10 pm during the week.
5. It would cost 4 DM for a child wanting to swim for a long time.
6. It would cost 10 DM if you wanted a sauna.
7. You could play mini-golf anytime between 10 am and 10 pm.
8. You would buy your ticket to play tennis at the swimming baths.

8 Going to the cinema

1. How many cinemas are there here?
2. What time is the last performance of Police Academy 4?
3. How many of the cinemas offer a late-night showing?
4. How many days in the week is the Asterix film on for?
5. Write down the name of the film you would see if your penfriend took you to the only early afternoon performance.

FILMCENTER UNNA · RUF 1 24 08

UNIVERSUM Kino 1	NEUES THEATER Kino 2	STUDIO Kino 3	MOVIE Kino 4
3. Woche	3. Woche	Michael Douglas, Kathleen Turner, Danny De Vito in	2. Woche
Der neueste Super-Hit mit EDDIE MURPHY – Der Auserwählte –	**POLICE ACADEMY 4** UND JETZT GEHT'S RUND!	**Auf der Jagd nach dem grünen Diamanten**	Adolf Winkelmanns neuester Film: **Peng Du bis tot**
AUF DER SUCHE NACH DEM GOLDENEN KIND		Do.-Mo. 16.30, 18.45, 21.00 Uhr Die. - Mi. 18.45, 21.00 Uhr Der neue Film des Pumuckl-Regisseurs Ulrich König:	mit Ingolf Lück – Rebecca Pauly Die Jagd nach dem Professor mit dem irren Prozessor Do.-Mo. 18.30 u. 20.45 Uhr Fr. u. Sa. 23.00 Uhr Spätvorstell.
Frei ab 12 Jahren Do.-Mo. 16.30, 18.45, 21.00 Uhr Die. - Mi. 18.45, 21.00 Uhr	Frei ab 6 Jahren Do.-Mo. 16.15, 18.30, 20.45 Uhr Die. - Mi. 18.30, 20.45 Uhr Fr. - Sa. 23.00 Uhr Spätvorstell.: **Monty Pythons: Das Leben des Brian**	**Hatschipuh** Freitag bis Sonntag 14.30 Uhr im Neuen Theater	5. Woche **Asterix bei den Briten** Do. bis Mo. täglich 16.15 Uhr

67

9 What's on TV?

ⅢNord

13.00 Internationale Tennismeisterschaften von Deutschland für Damen
Viertelfinale
Übertragung vom LTTC Rot-Weiß Berlin

18.00 Sesamstraße
Sendung für Kinder im Vorschulalter

18.30 Platzkonzert
Eine volksmusikalische Spurensuche im Oberharz mit Gerlind Rosenbusch (Wiederholung)

19.15 III INTERNATIONAL:
„Lieber Sammy..."
Briefe in die Todeszelle
Film von Angelika und Peter Schubert
Sammy Felder wartet seit acht Jahren im Todestrakt des Staatsgefängnisses Ellis in Huntsville/Texas auf seine Hinrichtung. Vor etwa zwei Jahren erfuhr Hausfrau Hildegard V. aus Deutschland von seinem Schicksal und begann einen intensiven Briefwechsel mit ihm.

20.00 Tagesschau/Wetter
(Videotext-Untertitel auf Tafel 150)

20.15 Die eigene Geschichte
„Muß es denn gleich beides sein?"
Aus dem Leben einer Aufsässigen
Hilde Radusch, Jahrgang 1903, erinnert sich an ihr ereignisreiches Leben.

21.00 Vor vierzig Jahren
British Movietone 885 vom 20. Mai 1946
Welt im Film 52 von 20. Mai 1946
Kommentar: Friedrich Luft
Der britische Beitrag berichtet ausführlich aus dem Fernen Osten, z. B. von den Kämpfen in Indonesien. Außerdem gibt es Filme über die Siegesparaden zum ersten Jahrestag der deutschen Kapitulation in Paris, Wien und Berlin. – „Welt im Film" zeigt Bilder von den Wahlen in Frankreich, vom Leben in Berlin, und Hans Albers ist in seiner Glanzrolle als Liliom zu sehen.

21.30 Der rote Engel
US-Spielfilm aus dem Jahr 1952
Roxy McClanahan (Yvonne de Carlo), Frank Truscott (Rock Hudson), Malcolm Bradley (Richard Denning), Linda Caldwell (Bodil Miller) u. a.
Regie: Sidney Salkow
Hauptattraktion in der Kneipe zum „Roten Engel" ist die schöne Roxy. Doch bei Kapitän Truscott hat sie kein Glück. Er durchschaut ihre Tricks. Dennoch hilft er ihr, als sie vor der Polizei fliehen muß. In einem Hotel hat Roxy eine Begegnung, die sie auf die Idee bringt, eine Dame der besseren Gesellschaft zu werden.

Yvonne de Carlo als Abenteurerin Roxy

22.50 „... und lieb sein kann ich auch"
Wolf Biermann und Eva-Maria Hagen
Live-Mitschnitt aus dem „Spiegelzelt"
12. Norddeutsches Theatertreffen 1982, Hamburg **(Wdh.)**
Es war das erste Fernseh-Konzert, das Wolf Biermann nach seinem sensationellen Vier-Stunden-Auftritt im November 1979 in Köln gegeben hat. Er und seine Freundin Eva-Maria Hagen singen Liebeslieder – von Biermann aus vielen Sprachen ins Deutsche „gezottelt", wie er sagt.

23.45 Nachrichten
Sendeschluß etwa 23.50

1 Your penfriend likes sport — which programme should he/she watch?
2 What time does it start?
3 You are interested in the weather forecast for tomorrow. When should you switch on?
4 How many news bulletins are there on this channel?
5 You like American films — until what time will you need to stay up to see the end of the one advertised here?

10 An evening out

Read this extract from a letter from a German family.

... Heute ist bei uns Maifeiertag, und wir genießen das schöne lange Wochenende. Da Arne so ein Fußballnarr ist und auch Maren sich dafür interessiert, fahren wir heute abend zu einem Bundesligaspiel nach Dortmund. Die Dortmunder spielen gegen den 1.FC Köln, Arnes Lieblingsverein. Die Kinder werden sicherlich überwältigt sein von der Stimmung in solch einem großen Stadion ...

1. To which day is the letter-writer referring?
2. Where is the family going?
3. Which club is Arne's favourite?
4. What does the writer say about the mood in the stadium and its effect on the children?

11 Acquiring a new skill

1. What could you learn to do here?
2. Who is the school especially for?
3. What is special about Wednesdays, Saturdays and Sundays?

TANZSCHULE

JEDE WOCHE DUFTE PARTYS! Zur Zeit mittwochs, samstags u. sonntags!

JUNG UND MODERN – LÜDENSCHEIDS TANZSCHULE FÜR SCHÜLERINNEN UND SCHÜLER

MEISTER

1 Hobbies

You will hear some German people talking about their hobbies. Fill in this table when you have listened to the recording.

Name	Hobby
Birgit	
Stefan	
Fatima	
Donato	

2 The Kiefer family

Herr Kiefer talks about his free time. Answer true or false to these statements.

1. Herr Kiefer leaves work at about half past five.
2. When he first gets in he has his tea.
3. In the summer he goes walking after work.
4. In the winter he likes watching television.
5. Sometimes in the evening he goes to the pub.
6. He goes bowling every Saturday.

Frau Kiefer talks about her hobby.

1. What does she like to do in her free time?
2. What does she particularly like to do at the weekend?

Beate talks about her hobby.

1. What does she like to do?
2. What is her favourite group?

3 An interview with a German assistant

1. Where and with whom does Barbara live?
2. In what kind of school is she working?
3. She says she plays squash — what other sports does she like?
4. Why does she find playing squash so much fun?
5. What does she say about her partner?
6. Name three things she likes to do in the evening.

4 Radio announcement

Listen to the recording, then answer true or false to these statements.

1. The Westfalen Park is in Dortmund.
2. There is a revolving restaurant there.
3. You can take a train ride or a chair lift to see more of the park.
4. There is mini-golf for children.
5. You can take the B1 road or the B45 to get to the park.

With a partner act out the following conversations taking it in turns to play each role.

1 Going swimming

You are making arrangements to go swimming with your penfriend.

Penfriend: Asks if you would like to go swimming.
You: Say you would like that very much.
Penfriend: Asks if you can swim well.
You: Say quite well, you go swimming once a week.
Penfriend: Asks what time you'd like to go.
You: Say about 3 pm.

2 Going to the cinema

You would like to go to the cinema. Ask your penfriend to go with you.

You: Ask if your penfriend would like to go to the cinema.
Penfriend: Asks what's on.
You: Say it's a thriller.
Penfriend: Asks what time it starts.
You: Say the first performance is at 7 pm.

3 My hobbies

Your penfriend's mother is asking you about your hobbies.

You:	Tell her you like sport and listening to music.
Mother:	Asks what kind of music you like listening to.
You:	Tell her pop music.
Mother:	Asks if you play a musical instrument.
You:	Tell her you play the guitar.

4 Declining an invitation: 1

Your penfriend's parents want to know if you would like to go out with them to see some friends.

You:	Say thank you very much, but you are tired.
Parents:	Suggest you watch television for a while.
You:	Say you would like to do that and ask what is on tonight.
Parents:	Tell you there is an English film on.
You:	Say you will watch it for a while.

5 Declining an invitation: 2

You meet a friend of your penfriend in Germany and this person asks you to go to the theatre tomorrow night. Unfortunately you are already going out with your penfriend's family. Explain this to the friend and suggest another evening.

6 A day trip

You have seen an advertisement in a travel agent's window for a day trip to Luxemburg from Traben-Trarbach, where you are staying with your penfriend. You would like to go on the trip, so you jot down the details and explain to your penfriend when you get back. Here are the details:

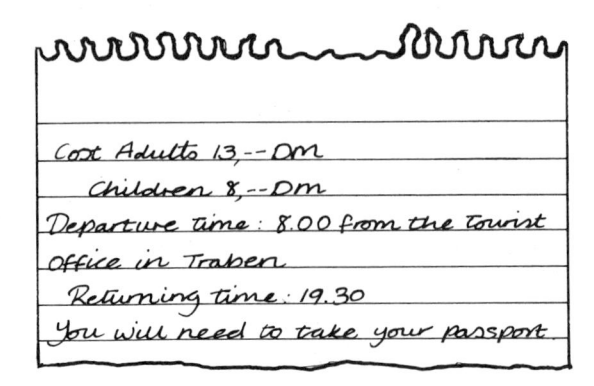

```
Cost Adults 13,--DM
     Children 8,--DM
Departure time: 8.00 from the Tourist
Office in Traben
Returning time: 19.30
You will need to take your passport
```

7 A talk on my hobbies

Prepare a one minute talk on your hobbies.

1 A message from my friend

You are alone in the house of your penfriend, when another friend calls round and asks you to go for a game of tennis. Leave a message for your penfriend saying where you have gone, who with and that you will be back about 6 pm.

2 A postcard

You are on holiday with your family. Send a postcard to your penfriend telling him/her that:

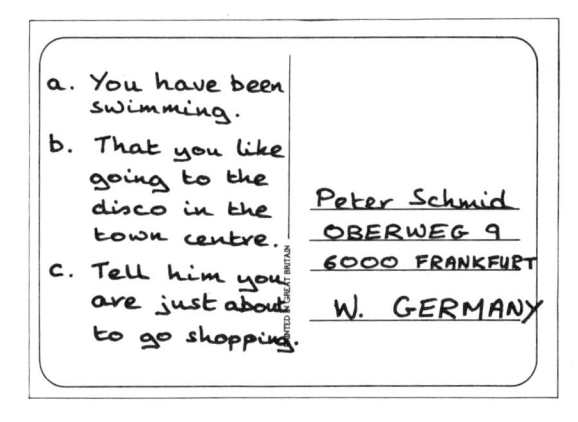

> a. You have been swimming.
> b. That you like going to the disco in the town centre.
> c. Tell him you are just about to go shopping.
>
> Peter Schmid
> OBERWEG 9
> 6000 FRANKFURT
> W. GERMANY

3 A letter about my hobbies

Write a short letter to your penfriend telling him about your hobbies and pastimes.

4 Spare time

You have been asked by your penfriend to write a piece for his/her class project on what English young people do in their spare time. Try to include as many things as you can in your account.

5 A letter to the tourist office

You are shortly going on holiday to the Black Forest area of Germany. Write to the tourist office in Freiburg explaining that you are very interested in walking, swimming and sailing. Ask them to send you some information about the area relating to these interests.

TOPIC 7: *Shopping, Food and Drink*

1 Shopping

You go shopping with your penfriend's family. Here is a list of what everyone wants. From which of the shops pictured here will you buy each item?

Item	Shop
Record	
Souvenirs	
Model train	
Shoes	
Pullover	
Leather gloves	

Männer mens Shop **Mode**
Hauptstraße 151 · 69 Heidelberg · Telefon 21364

allegri
Mäntel
Blousons

NINO CERRUTI
Anzüge
Saccos

valentino
Pullover

MISSONI
Strickjacken

LORENZINI
Hemden

Windsor
Hosen
Saccos
Anzüge

FENZI
Pullover

Edm. König

GmbH + Co KG

Hauptstraße 124
Universitätsplatz
Telefon 20929

Kristall - Porzellan
Kunstgewerbe-Souvenirs
in großer Auswahl

Hummel-Figuren

MEISSEN

Rosenthal

SCHALLPLATTEN kaufen Sie am besten bei KLAATU
Wir haben eine riesige Auswahl an Schallplatten und Musikkassetten in 2 Etagen. Ein Besuch lohnt sich. Wir sind die Spezialisten für Ihre Schallplatten.

KLAATU HEIDELBERG
Sophienstr. 9 – 69 Heidelberg

Haben Sie Schuhprobleme?
Möchten Sie trotz diffiziler Füße einen schicken Schuh tragen?
Wünschen Sie sich ein bestimmtes Modell, welches man in einem normalen Schuhgeschäft nicht findet?

Kommen Sie vorbei!

ITALIENISCHES Maß-Schuh-Atelier
● **Gavino + Marco**
Italienischer Schuhmachermeister
Italienischer Schuhmodellist

Wir lösen Ihre Probleme und erfüllen Ihre Wünsche.

6900 HD, Brückenstraße 34, 0 62 21 / 40 08 91

---

spiel + hobby

Das Geschäft für Modell-Eisenbahnen und Zubehör

Hauptstraße 192 · 69 Heidelberg
Telefon 06221/22780

Roco MODELLEISENBAHNEN

Leder Meid

HAUPTSTRASSE 88
TELEFON: 0 62 21 / 2 25 70
TÄGLICHE ÖFFNUNGSZEITEN:
Montag: 9.30-18.30 Uhr
Dienstag-Freitag: 9.00-18.30 Uhr
Kurze Samstage: 9.00-14.00 Uhr
Erster Samstag jeden Monats: 9.00-18.00 Uhr

Ihr Lederwaren-Spezialgeschäft im ♥ von Heidelberg
Tiefgarage C&A /P8

**Handtaschen · Handschuhe · Leder-Bekleidung
Gürtel · Schirme · Fluggepäck
Reiseartikel · Geschenkartikel**

Wir akzeptieren Kreditkarten (Diners, American Express, Visa, Eurocard)
Auf Wunsch versenden wir die bei uns gekaufte Ware für Sie.
Wir erledigen für Sie die mit einer MWSt.-Rückerstattung zusammenhängenden Formalitäten.

2 Buying an ice-cream

After all that shopping, you offer to buy everyone an ice-cream.

1 What flavours are available?
2 What would two coffee ice-creams, one mixed ice and a milk shake cost?

3 In the supermarket

These two photographs were taken inside the supermarket.

A 1 What are you asked to use here?
   2 What will happen at the cash desk if you don't?
   3 What should you not do if you are accompanied by young children?

B What is this warning notice about?

> **Diebstahl lohnt sich nicht!**
> Wir zeigen jeden Dieb an und verlangen Ersatz unseres Schadens.

4 A shopping centre

Look at this advertisement for a very large shop. Say which of these items are true.

1. This shop has five floors.
2. There are two parking areas.
3. You can buy goods from many foreign countries there.
4. It is the largest department store in Lüdenscheid.
5. The manager's name is Helmut Neuber.

Der **KAUFHOF** im CITY EINKAUFS CENTER LÜDENSCHEID

Sie finden in 8 Geschossen und 4 Verkaufsetagen
120 000 verschiedene Artikel aus 40 Ländern

470 Parkplätze stehen Kaufhof-Kunden in zwei Park-Decks zur Verfügung

Das größte Warenhaus in Lüdenscheid unter der Geschäftsführung von Herrn Helmut Neuber freut sich auf Ihren Besuch

Freu Dich auf den **KAUFHOF** Lüdenscheid
Der Kaufhof bietet tausendfach alles unter einem Dach

5 Eating out

As in any other city, Heidelberg has its fair share of foreign cuisine as well as German cuisine.

1. List the different kinds of restaurants on offer here.

Answer the following questions with the letters A–F.

2. Which restaurant recommends booking a table?
3. At which restaurant is English spoken?
4. You are going out with a friend. His favourite food is spaghetti, yours is kebabs. Which restaurant would cater for you both?
5. Which restaurant offers musical entertainment?
6. Where could you eat traditional German food?
7. Where could you get a lunch for less than 10 DM?

A

VIVA MEXICO

Mexikanische Spezialitäten · Türkische Spezialitäten
Griechische Spezialitäten · Italienische Spezialitäten

Tortillas, Enchiladas, Chili con Queso, Döner Kebap, Gyros
Pizza und Spaghetti

6900 Heidelberg 1
Am Theaterplatz · Hauptstr. 113A · Telefon 06221/28586

Geöffnet täglich durchgehend von 10.00 bis 24.00 Uhr

B

Stadtgarten

Café-Restaurant »DA ELIO«

Inhaber:
Fam. Nigrelli

Friedrich-Ebert-Anlage 2

69 Heidelberg

Telefon
06221/12805

Geöffnet:
10.30–24.00 Uhr
durchgehend

ITALIENISCHE SPEZIALITÄTEN

PIZZA

nach alter italienischer Tradition vom Holzofen
FISCHSPEZIALITÄTEN vom Holzkohlengrill

Biergarten
Im Ausschank:

DORTMUNDER UNION

Unser alkoholfreies Sortiment:
Mineral- und Tafelwässer,
Fruchtsäfte – von

Schaaff & Co

Heidelberg, Telefon 81007

C

Alte Gundtei
RESTAURANT · Inh. Fam. Kapli · G. Kozobolis

Türkische und Griechische Spezialitäten vom Holzkohlengrill

Türkische Atmosphäre mit Orig. Wein und Musik. Das Spitzenrestaurant in der Altstadt. Wir verwöhnen Sie mit unserer netten Bedienung. Alle Gerichte zum Mitnehmen. (Wir nehmen Reisebusse an). Reservierung empfohlen. Conferenzraum bis zu 70 Plätzen.

Prost Henninger!

Zwingerstr. 15a, Heidelberg, Tel. 06221/29395 · Tägl. 11-15 Uhr und 17.00-1.00 Uhr

D

Hackteufel

HOTEL-RESTAURANT-WEINSTUBE

DEUTSCHES SPEZIALITÄTENLOKAL
an der Alten Brücke

Steingasse 7
Telefon 06221/25589
P 12 + P 13

E

亞洲酒家

Schnell – gut – preiswert

Täglich verwöhnen wir unsere Gäste mit unserer reichlichen Auswahl an

Mittags-Menüs
Tagesgericht
incl. Vorspeise ab
8,- DM

CHINA RESTAURANT ASIA

Wir haben für Sie täglich geöffnet von 11.45-15.00 Uhr und von 17.45-24.00 Uhr. Samstag und Sonntag durchgehend geöffnet.

HEIDELBERG/ALTSTADT
an der Alten Brücke
Haspelgasse 2
Telefon 06221/29713

Gerne nehmen wir auch Ihre Tischreservierung entgegen.

F

Lord's Curry House
INDIAN RESTAURANT

Mittelbadgasse 3
6900 Heidelberg
Ecke Heiliggeistkirche
Telefon 062321/23236

Wir sprechen Englisch
Täglich Geöffnet:
17.00 - 24.00 Uhr

Wir akzeptieren AMERICAN EXPRESS

Kommt vorbei und probiert unsere Spezialitäten aus Indien
Lamm-, Rinder-, und Hühner-Curry, mit Safran Reis serviert

6 Out for a drink

Write in the correct prices for these drinks after consulting the drinks list.

Drink	Price
Pot of tea with milk or lemon	
Hot lemon drink	
A bottle of apple juice	
A bottle of cherry juice	
A bottle of beer	

1 What do you think *Bier vom Faß* is?
2 What does *Inklusivpreise* mean?

Warme Getränke	DM
Tasse *Jacobs*-Kaffee	1,90
Kännchen *Jacobs*-Kaffee	3,80
Tasse Kaffee entcoffeiniert	1,90
Kännchen Kaffee entcoffeiniert	3,80
Kännchen Mokka	4,80
Tasse Schokolade mit Sahne	2,00
Kännchen Schokolade mit Sahne	4,00
Glas Tee mit Milch oder Zitrone	1,90
Kännchen Tee mit Milch oder Zitrone	3,80
Irish Coffee	6,00
Russische Schokolade	6,00
Rüdesheimer Kaffee	7,50
Glas Grog mit Rum	3,00
Glas Tee mit Rum	3,50
Glas Glühwein, weiß oder rot	2,50
Heiße Zitrone	2,50
Espresso	2,00
Cappuccino	2,50

Den Wert unserer Gebäcke bestimmen die Zutaten!
Reiche Auswahl am Kuchenbuffet zu Tagespreisen.

— Inklusivpreise —

Alkoholfreie Getränke	DM
	0,20 *l*
Flasche Coca Cola	1,70
Flasche Fanta	1,70
Flasche Sprudel	1,50
Flasche Apfelsaft	1,80
Flasche Traubensaft	2,00
Flasche Kirschsaft	2,00
Flasche Orangensaft	2,00
Flasche Bitter Lemon	2,50

Bier vom Faß		
Bitburger Pils	0,30 *l*	2,40

Flaschenbiere	0,33 *l*
Bitburger Pils	2,50
Warsteiner Pilsener	2,50
Beck's Bier	2,50
Gatzweiler Alt	2,50
Malzbier	2,50

Damengedeck:
1 Likör nach Wahl und 1 Pikkolo   8,00

Herrengedeck:
1 Fl. Bier nach Wahl und 1 Pikkolo   8,00

— Inklusivpreise —

7 Cooking

Your penfriend has sent you this recipe, saying even he/she can make it!

1. What ingredients do you need?
2. How long do you bake the item for?

Das kann jeder

Heute: Pizza-Toast

"Für jeden gibt es 2 Toasts. Ich backe sie im Backofen bei 175° Grad (Celsius). Nach etwa 8 Minuten schmilzt der Käse. Dann sind sie fertig."

1 Scheibe Weißbrot mit Butter bestreichen.

Mit Tomatenscheiben belegen.

Salz, Pfeffer und Petersilie darüber streuen.

Mit Salami belegen.

Mit einer Scheibe Käse bedecken.

8 Making a pudding

Your penfriend has sent you his/her favourite dessert for you to make — vanilla pudding with chocolate sauce.

1. Write down briefly how you would make the vanilla pudding.
2. How would you make the chocolate sauce?
3. If you double the quantity of milk for the sauce what do the instructions say you will make?

FEINE DESSERTS

Dr. Oetker

Garant

Vanille-Geschmack

Puddingcreme-Pulver vollgezuckert für 500 ml Milch

Zubereitung:
1. 500 ml (1/2 l) Milch in einen Kochtopf gießen und zum Kochen bringen.
2. Den Topf von der Kochstelle nehmen, das Puddingcremepulver auf einmal unter Rühren mit einem Schneebesen in die Milch geben und etwa 1 Minute kräftig weiterrühren (den Topf nicht wieder auf die Kochstelle stellen).
Den Pudding in eine Glasschale oder in Portionsgläser füllen und erkalten lassen.

Tip:
Servieren Sie Garant Vanille-Geschmack mit einer feinen Soße, zubereitet mit Dr. Oetker Schokoladen-Soßen-Pulver oder Dr. Oetker Paradies-Soße Schokolade.

Zutaten:
Zucker, Stärke, modifizierte Stärke, Verdickungsmittel, Speisesalz, natürliche und naturidentische Aromastoffe, Trennmittel E 341, Farbstoffe E 102, E 110.

4 000521 250003

Dr. August Oetker, 4800 Bielefeld 1

Dr. Oetker

Probieren Sie doch mal die sahnig leichte Paradies-Soße

Schokoladen-Soßenpulver
für 250 ml (1/4 l) Milch
in 1 Minute fertig

1. 250 ml (1 4 l) Milch in eine große Schüssel gießen.

2. Den Inhalt des Päckchens auf einmal hinzufügen und sofort mit einem Schneebesen etwa 1 Minute schnell und kräftig durchschlagen, damit sich keine Klümpchen bilden.

Mit Dr. Oetker Soßenpulver Ohne Kochen zubereitete Soßen schmecken frisch am besten und sollten bald verzehrt werden.

Vorzüglich geeignet als Beigabe zu Vanille-, Mandel- oder Sahne-Pudding sowie zu Reis- und Grießspeisen. Unter Verwendung der doppelten Menge Milch (500 ml = 1/2 l) und etwas Zucker läßt sich ein köstliches Getränk zubereiten.

Zutaten: Zucker, Stärke, fettarmes Kakaopulver, Kochsalz, Vanillin.

Dr. August Oetker, 4800 Bielefeld 1

9 Salads

Your penfriend's mother has made some delicious salads whilst you have been staying there and you ask her for the recipes.

A Möhren-Weißkraut-Salat
  1 *Möhren* is another word for carrots — what other vegetable is used in this salad?
  2 Which four ingredients make up the dressing?

B Bunter Reis-Curry-Salat
  1 How long must you cook the rice for?
  2 How many onions do you need?
  3 What kind of fruit do you need for this salad?
  4 How many portions does this recipe make?

Möhren-Weißkraut-Salat — 4 Port.

250 g Möhren
250 g Weißkraut
5 Eßl. Weinessig
4 Eßl. Öl
1½ Eßl. Honig
1 Teel. Senf
1 Prise Selleriesalz
Petersilie

Möhren in dünne Stifte raffeln, Weißkraut fein hobeln und mit Essig in eine Schüssel geben, stampfen bis es weiches geworden ist. Dann Möhren, Öl, Honig, Senf und Selleriesalz darunter mischen und den Salat abschmecken. Mit gehackter Petersilie garnieren.

Dieser Salat ist als erfrischende Vorspeise oder als Beilage für andere Speisen geeignet.

Bunter Reis-Curry-Salat — 4 Port.

1 Tasse Reis, Salz
2 Zwiebeln
2 Eßl. Öl
1-2 Teel. Curry
250 g Schinkenwurst
2 Äpfel
2 Bananen
2 Gewürzgurken
1 Paprikaschote
1 Bund Schnittlauch
¼ l Sahne (steif geschlagen)
Zitronensaft
Salz, Pfeffer

Reis 16 Min. kochen, abgießen u. abschmecken. Gewürfelte Zwiebeln in Öl hell andünsten und mit Curry verrühren. Reis und Zwiebeln in einer Salatschüssel mischen. Wurst, geschälte u. entkernte Äpfel, Bananen, Gurken u. entkernte Paprikaschote in kleine Stücke schneiden, Schnittlauch hacken. Alle geschnittenen Zutaten zum Reis geben. Die geschlagene Sahne mit Zitronensaft, Salz und Pfeffer verrühren. Den Salat damit anmachen. Durchziehen lassen, nochmals abschmecken.

Als reichlicher Partysalat zu empfehlen!

10 Something to eat

Look carefully at the menu on this and the next page and decide which of these statements are true or false.

1. There are five kinds of soup on offer.
2. With each bowl of soup you get a bread roll.
3. The chicken soup has cream in it.
4. You can buy a cheese sandwich here.
5. A curry sausage would cost 4,20 DM.
6. The Hungarian goulash is served with vegetables and rice.

Schnelle Snacks:	
Pizza Schnitte Salami	3,--
Heiße Hexe Hamburger	3,--
Heiße Hexe Cheeseburger	3,50
Heiße Hexe Frikadellen mit Brot	3,50
Heiße Hexe Currywurst	3,50
Champignon Baguette	3,50
Pizza "Bella Napoli"	5,50
3 Rindsbockwürstchen mit Brötchen	4,20
2 Riesenbockwürste mit Brötchen	5,20
Portion Rostbratwürstchen mit Brot	5,50
Schlachtfest:	
Bauchspeck, Blut und Leberwurst mit Salzkartoffeln	9,90
Kasseler Rauchwurst, Grünkohl mit Salzkartoffeln	10,20
Tellergerichte	
Ungarisch Gulasch mit Gemüse und Salzkartoffeln	11,90
Hühnerfrikasse mit Reis "Frühlingsart"	10,50

Heiße Süppchen mit Brötchen:

Bouillon	2,50
Hühnersuppe mit Ei	3,50
Gulaschsuppe	3,80
Bihunsuppe "Bali"	3,80
Mexikanische Bohnensuppe	3,80

EINTÖPFE: Portion zum Sattessen
mit Brot oder Brötchen

Kartoffelsuppe mit 2 Würstchen	5,90
Erbseneintopf mit 2 Würstchen	6,20
Grüne Bohnen Eintopf mit Rindfleisch	6,50

Belegte Brote: reichlich garniert

mit Holländer Käse	5,50
mit feiner Cervelatwurst	5,50
mit Schwarzwälder Bauernspeck	5,50
mit Schwarzwälder Bauernschinken	6,--
Restaurationsschnittchen "Cafe Mayer"	7,--

1 Shopping

A You are in the supermarket and hear the following announcement:
1 What item is on offer?
2 How much does it cost?

B You ask for some ham in a shop, but don't get the answer you expect.
You say: *6 Scheiben gekochten Schinken.*
What does the assistant reply?

C You go to the local baker to buy some bread rolls with your penfriend. When he/she asks for the rolls, you hear the following reply.
What two things is he/she told?

D You go to the butcher to buy a kilo of *Bratwurst*. The assistant then asks you this question.
What does she want to know?

E You buy some salami and some *Bockwurst* and ask the cost.
How much do you have to pay altogether?

2 Favourite things

You ask your German friends about what they like to eat and drink. Here are their replies:

	Likes	Dislikes
1		
2		
3		
4		
5		

3 Staying with a penfriend

It is nearly dinner-time and you ask your penfriend's mother if you can help her.

1 What does she reply?
2 You ask her where the plates are. Where are they?
3 You ask her what there is to eat. What is there?
4 Now she asks you something. What does she want to know?
5 You ask if there is a dessert. What is her answer?

4 Guests for dinner

Your penfriend's father has invited some friends to dinner at the weekend. He discusses the arrangements with his wife.

1. For what night has the invitation been issued?
2. Why does his wife complain?
3. How does he offer to help?
4. What will they have for starters?
5. Why can't she serve fish as the main course?
6. What vegetables will they serve?
7. What will there be for dessert?
8. What will they have to drink and why?

With a partner act out the following conversations taking it in turns to play each role.

1 At the baker

Assistant:	Asks what you would like.
You:	Say you would like six bread rolls.
Assistant:	Asks if you would like anything else.
You:	Say you would like a white loaf.
Assistant:	Gives it to you.
You:	Ask how much it costs altogether.
Assistant:	Tells you.

2 At the butcher

Butcher: Asks if he can help you.
You: Say you would like 250 g of *Bierwurst*.
Butcher: Asks if that is all.
You: Ask for four slices of ham and ask the cost.
Butcher: Tells you.

3 At the fruit shop

Assistant: Asks if you want any help.
You: Ask for six bananas.
Assistant: Asks if you want anything else.
You: Ask if they have any apples.
Assistant: Says they have red apples and green apples.
You: Ask for four red apples.

4 In the department store

You want to buy a tie for your father.

You: Ask where the men's department is.
Assistant: Tells you it is on the second floor.
You: *You pick a tie.* Ask where you have to pay.
Assistant: Tells you to pay at the cash desk.

5 Buying a pullover

While you are there you decide to buy a pullover.

You: Say you would like a pullover.
Assistant: Asks what size.
You: Say you would like a 42.
Assistant: Asks what colour.
You: Say blue.
Assistant: Says they have only red and green in your size.
You: Ask to try the green one on.

6 Shopping for a present

You go shopping for a present for your mother. You have 20 DM to spend, but do not want to buy chocolates because your mother does not eat sweets, and you don't want to buy perfume because you have forgotten which fragrance she likes. Ask the shop assistant to help find a present for under 20 DM.

What will you say if she offers you chocolates or perfume as possible presents?

7 Buying a T-shirt

You go shopping for a T-shirt for your brother aged ten years. His favourite colour is blue, but he detests red. You want to pay about 12 DM. What would you say to the assistant?

8 Shopping for a party

Your penfriend is having a party for a few friends. You offer to help with the shopping. Find out how many people are coming and what you should buy to eat. Also, what there is to drink.

9 In the café: 1

You: Call the waitress over.
Waitress: Asks what you would like.
You: Order a cup of coffee with milk and a cup of tea.
Waitress: Asks if you would like anything to eat.
You: Order a piece of cheesecake.

10 In the café: 2

You: Call the waiter over.
Waiter: Asks what you would like.
You: Order a lemon tea and a coke.
Waiter: Asks if you would like something to eat.
You: Say nothing, thank you. Ask for the bill.

11 In the restaurant: 1

You: Ask the waiter for a menu.
The waiter brings it to you.
You: Ask what he recommends.
Waiter: Says the *Schnitzel* is very good.
You: Order *Schnitzel* with chips and peas.
Waiter: Asks what you would like to drink.
You: Order a glass of mineral water.

12 In the restaurant: 2

You: Ask for a table for two near the window.
The waiter shows you to your table.
You: Ask for the menu.
The waiter brings it for you.
You: Ask what the soup of the day is.
Waiter: Tells you it is vegetable soup.

13 Booking a table

You wish to reserve a table in a restaurant for that evening at 8 pm. Telephone the restaurant and book a table for four. Give your name and say it will be a birthday celebration.

14 A complaint

You have just eaten a meal in a restaurant along with the rest of your family. Unfortunately it was not a very nice meal — the vegetables were cold, the meat was over-cooked and the potatoes were salty. Call the waiter over and make a complaint.

1 Filling in a card

You have just eaten in this snack bar and decide to fill in this card about your meal. Say:

1 The waitress was very pleasant.
2 The food was good and hot.
3 The strawberry ice-cream was delicious.

Complete any other details asked for on the card.

WILLKOMMEN BEI ALBERTO'S

Vielen Dank für ihren Besuch

Wir hoffen, dass wir Sie gut bedient haben

wünscht Ihnen das Personal

Bitte geben Sie ihr Urteil an, über unseren Servis, danke.

WIR TUN DAS BESTE
DEUTSCHER IMBISS
FÜR SIE

Datum: .... Uhr-Zeit ....

GUTEN APPETIT

2 A postcard

You are on a school trip staying in a Youth Hostel. Send a postcard to your penfriend saying:

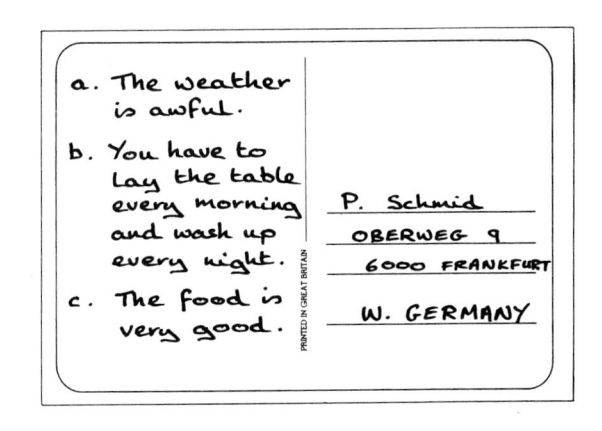

a. The weather is awful.
b. You have to lay the table every morning and wash up every night.
c. The food is very good.

P. Schmid
OBERWEG 9
6000 FRANKFURT
W. GERMANY

94

3 A shopping list

Your penfriend's mother is going shopping and offers to get anything you need — as long as you make a list for her.

1. Say you would like a tube of toothpaste and some soap.
2. Thank her and say you will pay her when she gets back.

4 A message

Your penfriend is at school and you want to go out. In case you are still out when your penfriend gets back from school you leave a note, saying:

1. You are going into town to buy a present for your mother.
2. You are also going to the museum.
3. You will be back about 3.30 pm.

5 Letter to a penfriend

Write a letter to your penfriend saying you have just been out shopping and have bought some new shoes. Say you have also bought a record. Say where you bought the things and describe them. Ask if your penfriend often goes shopping.

6 A day in town

You go with a friend to spend a day in a large city near your home. You do some shopping in the morning, have lunch in a restaurant and then have a look around the shops again in the afternoon. Write a letter to your friend describing your day.

7 A birthday meal

It is your birthday next week and you are planning to go with a group of friends for a meal to celebrate. Write about your plans to your penfriend — say what you did on your last birthday and ask your friend how he/she celebrates a birthday.

TOPIC 8: Around the Town

1 Signs and notices

1 Where would you get to if you followed this sign?

2 What activity is forbidden here?

3 And here?

4 What are you asked to do here and why?

5 This car park is open to the public at particular times only.
   a   When exactly?
   b   What might happen to your car if you disobey the instructions?

PRIVATPARKPLATZ

Nur für Bedienstete der Kreisverwaltung Cochem-Zell
mit besonderem
PARKAUSWEIS
Anderen Personen ist das Parken von 16.00 Uhr bis
7.00 Uhr morgens, an Feiertagen und Wochenenden
zeitlich uneingeschränkt gestattet.
Nichtberechtigt parkende Kraftfahrzeuge werden
kostenpflichtig abgeschleppt.

Kreisverwaltung Cochem-Zell
in Cochem

6   What are you requested to do here?

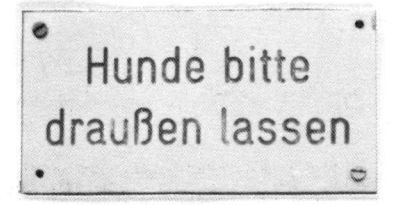

Hunde bitte
draußen lassen

7   And here?

Türe schließen

8   What are you asked to do here and why?

Arzt
Ausfahrt bitte Tag und
Nacht freihalten !

9   What is a *Fußgängerzone*?
    Which people have access to this area at any time?

> **Fußgängerzone**
>
> Be- und Entladen
> frei für Zulieferer
>
> von 6-10 h
>   18.30-20 h
>
> für Hotelgäste
> von 0-24 h

10   If you followed these signs where would you get to?

> Cusanus-Krankenhaus
>
> Postamt
> Polizei

2 A tour of the town

1 When and at what time do these visits take place?
2 Exactly where should you meet if you want to take part?

Führungen DURCH DEN HISTORISCHEN STADTKERN VON **Bernkastel-Kues**

JEDEN DONNERSTAG 15.30 Uhr

Treffpunkt: JEWEILS IN BERNKASTEL AM TURM DER ST. MICHAELS KIRCHE

3 Town library

1 When is half-day closing at the library in Corneliusstraße?
2 For how long is this branch usually closed at lunch time?
3 On which days of the week is the Rathausplatz branch closed all day?

Stadtbücherei
Lüdenscheid
Corneliusstraße 44
Öffnungszeiten:

Mo	10.00–13.00	15.00–18.30 Uhr
Di	10.00–13.00	15.00–18.30 Uhr
Mi	10.00–13.00	– – Uhr
Do	10.00–13.00	15.00–18.30 Uhr
Fr	– –	15.00–18.30 Uhr
Sa	10.00–12.30	– – Uhr

Wir seh'n uns in der Stadtbücherei

Stadtbücherei
Lüdenscheid
Zweigstelle Mediothek
Rathausplatz 10 – Tel. 1 74 75
Öffnungszeiten:

Mo 12.30–18.00 Uhr
Di 12.30–18.00 Uhr
Mi 10.00–12.00 Uhr
Do 12.30–18.00 Uhr
Fr 12.30–18.00 Uhr

4 Church services

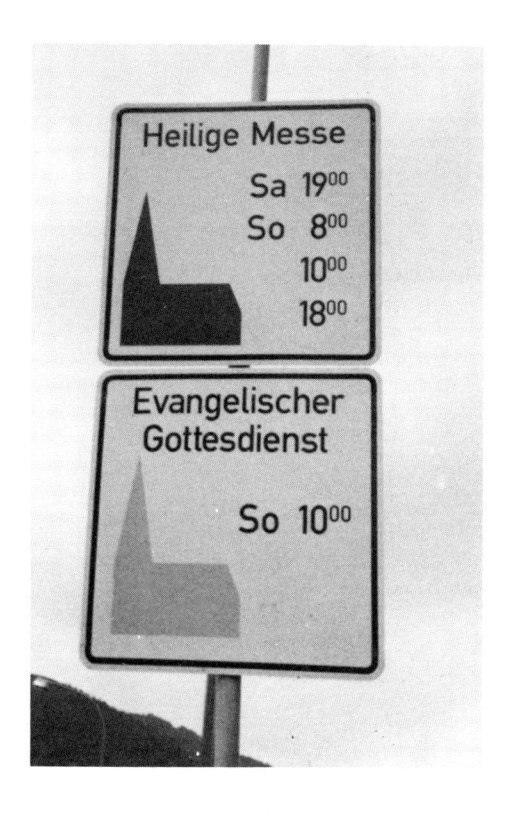

1. How many services are there at the Catholic church on Sundays?
2. What time does the Protestant church service begin?

Heilige Messe
Sa 19:00
So 8:00
10:00
18:00

Evangelischer Gottesdienst
So 10:00

5 Information service

You have just arrived in Frankfurt where you are to spend part of your summer holiday. You want to go to the information office to get some details about the city. You see this notice.

Informationsstellen
Information service

Informationsbüros:
Im Hauptbahnhof, Nordseite,   23 22 18
gegenüber Gleis 23   ⟨23 10 55⟩
geöffnet: 1.4.–31.10. werktags 8.00–22.00 Uhr,
sonn- und feiertags 9.30–20.00 Uhr.
geöffnet: 1.11.–31.3. werktags 8.00–21.00 Uhr,
sonn- und feiertags 9.30–20.00 Uhr.

Frankfurter Verkehrsverein e. V.   25 27 37
Offizielle Gästebetreuungsstelle
der Stadt Frankfurt am Main
Geschäftsleitung: Gutleutstraße 7–9
Telex 412 610 fvvev d

Hauptwache-Passage   28 74 86
geöffnet: werktags 9.00–18.00 Uhr,
            samstags 9.00–14.00 Uhr,
            sonntags geschlossen.

1. Exactly where is the information office in the station?
2. When will the office be open during the time of your visit to the city?

6 Heidelberg

Read this article, then decide which of the statements are true or false.

EINKAUFEN IN HEIDELBERG

Einkaufen in Heidelberg ist attraktiv:

Das Angebot übertrifft in seiner Vielfalt die kühnsten Erwartungen, und auf einem einzigen Einkaufsbummel zu Fuß kann man alle Einkäufe erledigen.

Im Bereich um die Fußgängerzone mit den vielen kleinen Straßen, auf hübschen Marktplätzen findet man zahllose Läden, Geschäfte und Boutiquen mit größter Auswahl: Porzellan, Glas und Schmuck, Möbel, Kleidung – bis hin zu Autos.

Hier leben Tradition und Moderne nebeneinander, hier gibt es alte etablierte Firmen, kleine Läden ebenso wie große Kaufhäuser, wie Kaufhof, Horten, C+A und die Kaufhalle. Gleich daneben finden Sie die Boutiquen.

Antiquariate, Briefmarkenläden und die Antiquitätengeschäfte locken zum Anschauen.

Um sich einen Überblick zu verschaffen, bietet Heidelberg täglich um 10.00 und 14.00 Uhr eine Stadtrundfahrt, die vom Bismarckplatz ausgeht. Die Dauer der Stadtrundfahrt liegt bei 2 1/2 Stunden.

Das Zentrum ist die Heidelberger Altstadt.

Unternehmen Sie eine Altstadtwanderung und lernen Sie die vielen kleinen Gassen nahe der Heiliggeist-Kirche kennen. Hier finden Sie viele Antiquitätenläden, die zum Anschauen und Einkaufen locken. Antiquitätenliebhaber sind hier an der richtigen Adresse.

Möchten Sie über die Heidelberger Hauptstraße bummeln, werden Sie unterwegs eine große Auswahl gemütlicher Gaststätten und Restaurants entdecken. Hier können Sie gut und preiswert zu Mittag essen.

Am Nachmittag empfehlen wir eine Kaffeepause in den bekannten Heidelberger Cafés (»Schafheutle«, mit seinem einladenden Gartenhof – Markt 7 – Victoria Café), um nur einige zu nennen.

Hauptstraße
(Fußgängerzone)

1 This article is mainly about shopping in Heidelberg.
2 Heidelberg is a good town for pedestrians because there are many car-free areas.
3 You could easily find shops selling clothes and jewellery here.
4 There is a tour of the town at 10 am and at 4 pm.
5 The tour leaves from the station.
6 The tour lasts for half an hour.
7 Many shops in the old town sell antiques.
8 Many of the restaurants are to be found in the main street.
9 The article suggests that you try one of Heidelberg's cafés in the afternoon.

1 Freiburg

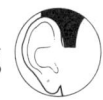

1 What reason does this person give for living in Freiburg?
2 Where in Germany is the town of Freiburg?
3 How does this person describe Freiburg?
4 Does she like living here?
5 What does she like doing in summer?
6 What does she like doing in winter?

2 Frankfurt

Which of these statements are true?

1 This person lives south of the town centre.
2 The city is big and modern.
3 *Die Zeil* is a wide street lined with shops.
4 Frankfurt has a large station on the outskirts of the city.

3 Directions

You probably know very well how to ask the way in German, but can you understand the replies? Imagine you have just asked the way to these places. Say exactly what information you have been given.

1

2

3

4

5

4 Situations

Listen carefully to these recordings of situations you might find yourself in, were you to visit Germany. Answer the questions.

1. You are in a café in Germany and order a piece of cake. What does the waitress ask you?
2. You are in a baker's shop and have just asked for a loaf of white bread. What does the shop assistant ask?
3. You have lost your wallet and go to the police station to report it. What does the policeman want to know?
4. You stop a passer-by and ask your way to the museum. What does she tell you?
5. You are at the station. The official tells you that the train for Cologne leaves in ten minutes. What else does he tell you?
6. You are at the Youth Hostel. You have given the warden your name. What does he then ask you?
7. You are in a restaurant and have ordered your meal. What does the waiter ask?
8. You are in a bank changing traveller's cheques. What does the clerk ask?
9. You have bought some soap for yourself and some toothpaste and a toothbrush for your penfriend. How much did the toothpaste and brush cost?
10. You ask your penfriend if he wants to go swimming. He says he can't. Why?

With a partner act out the following conversations taking it in turns to play each role.

1 Your hometown

You meet a friend of your penfriend who wants to know something about your home town. He/she asks you some questions.

Friend: Asks where you live.
You: Say where you live.
Friend: Asks if it is a small town.
You: Say how big your town/village is.
Friend: Asks what there is to do there.
You: Say there is a cinema and a youth club there.

2 Sport in your town

Your penfriend is looking forward to visiting you in the summer. He/she is particularly interested in sport and wants to know what sports he/she can play in your town.

Penfriend: Asks if there is a swimming pool.
You: Say there are two swimming pools — an indoor and an outdoor one.
Penfriend: Asks where you can play tennis.
You: Say you play at school and also in the park.

3 Shopping in your town

Imagine you live in a small town or village where the shopping facilities could be better. Your penfriend asks you these questions.

Penfriend: Asks if you often go shopping.
You: Say that the town is very small and the shops are not very good.
Penfriend: Asks where you buy your clothes.
You: Say you go to the next town.
Penfriend: Asks how you get there.
You: Say you go by bus or with your parents in the car.

4 Asking the way: 1

You are in town and want to know where the nearest bank is. You stop a passer-by.

You: Say excuse me and ask where the nearest bank is.
Passer-by: Tells you.
You: Ask her to repeat it more slowly please.
Passer-by: Does so.
You: Thank him/her.

5 Asking the way: 2

This time you need to know how to get to the museum.

You: Say excuse me and ask how to get to the museum.
Passer-by: Tells you.
You: Ask if it's far.
Passer-by: Tells you.
You: Say thank you.

6 Your home town

Be prepared to talk in detail about your home town. You should know how to give the following information in German:

Where your home town is. How old it is. How many people live there. What there is to do there. Whether it is an industrial town. If it's famous for anything — if so what?

Plus anything else of interest about the area in which you live.

7 An interview

You are writing a piece for your school magazine about the town where your penfriend lives. You decide to interview your penfriend. Make a list of all the questions you could ask and try them out on a partner — but make sure you can answer them yourself!

1 A postcard from London

You are on a day trip to London from school to see the museums. Send a postcard to your penfriend saying:

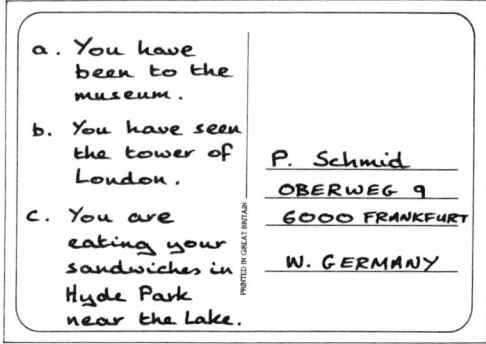

a. You have been to the museum.
b. You have seen the tower of London.
c. You are eating your sandwiches in Hyde Park near the lake.

P. Schmid
OBERWEG 9
6000 FRANKFURT
W. GERMANY

2 A postcard from your town

You send your penfriend a postcard of your home town.

1 Say your house is only five minutes from the town centre.
2 Say there are many shops and two cinemas.
3 Say in the evening you go swimming in the indoor pool.

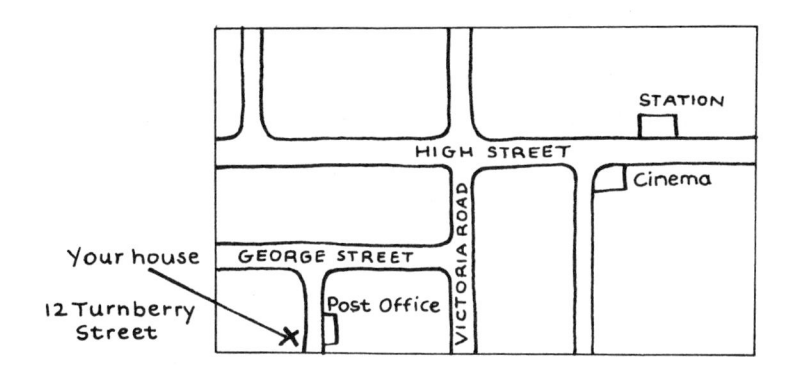

3 Directions

Your penfriend is staying with you. A friend of his/hers is visiting a nearby town and suggests spending the day with you. He/she will arrive by train, but is not sure at what time. To avoid waiting around, you decide to send him/her directions to your house from the station. Look at the map above and give the directions in German in as much detail as you can.

4 Where you live

You have just started writing to a German person. Write a letter telling him/her all about your town and whether or not you like living there, and why.

5 A letter to the tourist office

You are hoping to spend some time in Heidelberg during the summer holidays. Write to the Tourist Information Office there requesting a town plan, some information about the town itself, places of interest to visit, and a list of places to stay.

TOPIC 9: *At Your Service*

1 Changing money

A You arrive in the German town where you are to spend a few days. At the station you pick up a leaflet about banks.

> **A** **Geldwechsel**
> **Change**
>
> **Deutsche Verkehrs-Kredit-Bank AG**
> Hauptbahnhof, Südausgang   2 64 82 01
> geöffnet: täglich von 6.30 – 22.00 Uhr.
>
> Hauptbahnhof-Passage   2 64 82 41
> geöffnet: täglich von 8.00 – 20.00 Uhr.
>
> Flughafen   6 90 35 06
> geöffnet: täglich von 7.30 – 21.30 Uhr.

1 In how many places can you change money at the station?
2 Until what time at night can you change money?
3 At what other place in the town can you change money?

B

DVKB-Wechselstuben in großen Bahnhöfen, in Flughäfen, an Grenzübergängen.

Ihre Partner für Auslandsreisen:

○ ausländische Währungen und Reiseschecks.
○ Bargeld gegen eurocheques und Kreditkarten.

Problemlos und schnell. Bis spätabends.
Meist auch sonntags.

REISEGELD FÜR ALLE WELT

DEUTSCHE VERKEHRS-KREDIT-BANK

B   1   This bank advertises money changing facilities in stations, airports and where else?
    2   How many days a week are most of the banks open?

2 To the doctor

1   Which doctor has no surgery on Wednesday afternoon?
2   Which doctor has an appointment system?
3   Which doctor specializes in treating children?

Dr. med. Klobe
Kinderarzt
Allergologie

Sprechzeiten 9-12 Uhr
nachmittags nach Vereinbarung
Tel   Alle Kassen

Dr. med. Hartmut Mühle
Arzt
für Allgemeinmedizin

Sprechzeiten: Mo – Fr.   8-11
                     Mo.   nachm. 16-18
                     Di. Do. Fr. nachm. 16-17

3 Take note

This photograph was taken in an hotel cloakroom.
What does the sign ask you to do?

Wir bitten auf Ihre Garderobe selbst zu achten, da wir für entstehenden Schaden nicht haften.

4 Lost property

When exactly is the lost property office open?

FUNDBÜRO
WERKTAGS
8 – 12 – UHR
14 – 17 – UHR
SAMSTAGS
8 – 12 – UHR

5 Telephoning Germany

Your penfriend has not received a letter from you for ages! In desperation he/she has sent you this card, which explains how to telephone Germany.

1. Explain how, according to the card, you would make a call to Germany.
2. With which service would you be connected if you telephoned the number at the bottom of the card?

Ruf doch mal an!

Die Telefon-Information für Großbritannien-Reisende.

So einfach ist es, zu Hause anzurufen: Von öffentlichen Telefonen, in gekennzeichneten Privatgeschäften und von Telefonzellen.

Zuerst die Vorwahlnummer 0 10 49 der Bundesrepublik Deutschland wählen.

Dann die Ortsnetzkennzahl ohne die erste 0. Für Düsseldorf also nicht 0211, sondern 211.

Dann die Anschlußnummer des Teilnehmers. Probieren Sie es aus – z.B. mit dem Nachrichtendienst in Düsseldorf: 0 10 49/211/11 65.

6 Problems?

**Fragen, Probleme, Sorgen?
Ruf uns an. Wir hören zu.

Sorgentelefon
für Kinder Mo-Fr 14-19h
☎ 467777**

1 To whom is this telephone service available?
2 On which days and between which times is the telephone line open?

7 Post

This leaflet has been delivered to houses in Germany along with the post.

Sie lieben Ihren Hund

... und Sie lieben es auch, Ihre Post daheim zu erhalten

Ihr Briefträger möchte gerne Ihre Post zustellen und sie Ihnen, falls nötig, auch persönlich übergeben können, ohne einen Unfall zu riskieren.

Wissen Sie, daß jährlich fast 3.000 Briefträger der Deutschen Bundespost während ihres Zustellganges Opfer bissiger Hunde werden?

Gewöhnen Sie Ihren Hund an den Besuch Ihres Briefträgers.

1. What is the leaflet about?
2. What is the instruction at the bottom of the leaflet?

1 A visit to the doctor

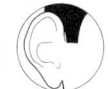

You have not been feeling well and go to the doctor. He asks you some questions.

1   What does he ask you first?

You explain you have been feeling very sick and have a bad stomach ache.

2   What does he ask now?

He gives you a prescription.

3   What does he tell you to do?

Dr. med. Hartmut Mühle
Arzt
für Allgemeinmedizin

Sprechzeiten: Mo. – Fr.   8 – 11
Mo.   nachm. 16 – 18
Di. Do. Fr. nachm. 16 – 17

2 Feeling ill

Rolf comes down to breakfast one morning and is obviously not feeling very well. The following conversation takes place between him and his mother.

1   Of what does Rolf complain?
2   What does his mother ask?
3   What does she tell him to do?

3 At the bank

This conversation takes place in the bank.

1   What does the customer want to do?
2   Why does this prove to be impossible?
3   At what time does the bank close?

4 At the Post Office

Complete this table about what this person buys at the Post Office.

Number of stamps	
Cost per stamp	
For postcards or letters	

5 At the Lost Property Office

Listen to the recording, then say which of these statements are true or false.

1. The man's first name is Peter.
2. The number of his house is 24.
3. His telephone number is 33 61 62.
4. He works in an office in town.
5. He has lost a brown leather wallet.
6. It contained a small notebook.
7. He lost it at mid-day.
8. He lost it in front of the cinema.
9. The lady finally asks him to sign the form she has just filled in.

With a partner act out the following conversations taking it in turn to play each role.

1 At the Post Office

You go to the Post Office to buy some stamps.

You:	Ask how much it costs to send a letter to England.
Assistant:	Tells you 80 Pf.
You:	Ask for three stamps at 80 Pf.

2 At the bank

You go to the bank to change a traveller's cheque.

You:	Say you would like to change a traveller's cheque.
Assistant:	Asks you for your passport.
You:	Hand it over.
Assistant:	Asks you to sign the cheque.
You:	You do so and ask what the exchange rate is today.
Assistant:	Tells you it is 2,90 DM, and asks you to go to the cash desk.
You:	Say thank you.

3 At the chemist

You have not been feeling too well, so you go with your penfriend's mother to the chemist.

You:	Tell the chemist you have a headache and a sore throat.
Chemist:	Asks you how long you have been feeling ill.
You:	Say since yesterday morning.
Chemist:	Sells you some tablets.
You:	Ask when you should take them.
Chemist:	Tells you three times a day after meals.

4 At the hospital

You have hurt your arm and banged your head whilst skiing and have been taken to the hospital.

Doctor:	Asks what you have been doing.
You:	Say you were skiing and you fell.
Doctor:	Asks where it hurts most.
You:	Say your hand is very painful.
Doctor:	Asks if that is all.
You:	Say you have a bad headache and feel sick.

5 No school today

Your penfriend is not well and is unable to go with you on the trip that has been organized for that day. Your penfriend's father takes you to school and asks you to explain to the teacher.

Teacher:	Asks where your friend is.
You:	Say he/she has stomach ache and diarrhoea.
Teacher:	Says he/she is very sorry.
You:	Say he/she has taken some tablets.
Teacher:	Asks when he/she will be back at school.
You:	Say tomorrow morning.

6 A lost bag

You have lost your sports bag after a visit to the local swimming baths in the German town where you are staying. You went to the café on the way home and think you might have left the bag there. You go back to the café to find out. The bag is red, has your sports clothes in and your name on the inside. Explain to a waitress what has happened. You should be prepared to describe the bag and its contents and find out what you should do next, if it is not there.

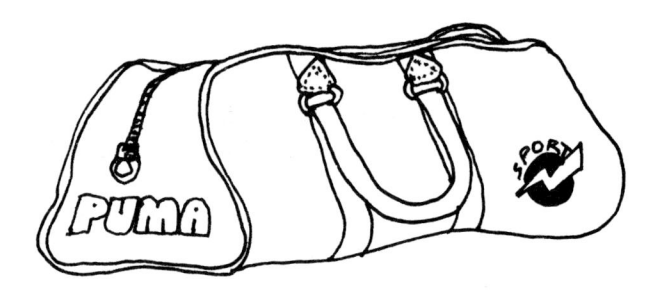

7 At the dentist

You have toothache and visit the dentist.

You:	Ask for an appointment.
Receptionist:	Suggests next Tuesday.
You:	Ask if you could see the dentist today.
Receptionist:	Says he/she is very busy.
You:	Say you have very bad toothache.

You are shown in to the dentist.

Dentist:	Asks you which tooth hurts.
You:	Say one at the top, on the left side.
Dentist:	Says you will need an injection.
You:	Say that's all right.

1 A telephone message

You take a telephone message for your penfriend's brother, Bernd, from a friend. He asks you to give Bernd a message when he returns home, saying:

1. He cannot go out because he has had an accident.
2. He has fallen and hurt his leg.
3. He will telephone again tomorrow.

2 In hospital

Your penfriend has written to say he/she would like a letter from you as soon as you have time to write, as he/she is in hospital with a broken leg and is bored. Write a reply saying:

1. Thank you for his/her letter.
2. You are sorry to hear about his/her broken leg.
3. Ask how he/she broke the leg.
4. Tell him/her you once broke your arm, but did not stay in hospital.
5. Say you will write again soon.

3 A lost jacket

Whilst you were staying with your penfriend, you left behind a jacket. Write a letter to your penfriend saying:

1. Thank you for your stay — you had a great time.
2. Ask him/her if by chance he/she has found your jacket — a blue one, which you left in the cupboard in the bedroom.
3. Ask if he/she could send the jacket to you.
4. Say you will send the money for the stamps.

4 A lost rucksack

Whilst youth hostelling in Germany, you left behind a small rucksack in the Bonn Hostel. Write to the Youth Hostel warden explaining this. Describe the rucksack and say what was in it.

5 An accident

You were due shortly to visit your penfriend for a holiday, but will not now be able to do so, as you have broken your arm and have to go to the hospital every week. In a letter to your friend, explain your problem and also how the accident happened.